LIONEL TRILLING

E. M. FORSTER

Oxford Melbourne
OXFORD UNIVERSITY PRESS
1982

Oxford University Press, Walton Street, Oxford OX2 6DP

OXFORD LONDON GLASGOW
NEW YORK TORONTO MELBOURNE WELLINGTON
KUALA LUMPUR SINGAPORE HONG KONG TOKYO
DELHI BOMBAY CALCUTTA MADRAS KARACHI
NAIROBI DAR ES SALAAM CAPE TOWN

Published by arrangement with Harcourt Brace Jovanovich, Inc.
First published in UK by The Hogarth Press Ltd. 1967
First published by Oxford University Press 1982

Acknowledgment

The extensive quotations from A Passage to India, Goldsworthy Lowes
Dickinson and Abinger Harvest are used by the courtesy of and by special
arrangement with Harcourt Brace Jovanovich and those from Where Angels Fear
to Tread, The Longest Journey, A Room with a View and Howards End
are used by the courtesy of and by special arrangement with Alfred A. Knopf, Inc.
The first chapter of this book appeared, in somewhat different form, as an essay in
The Kenyon Review and it is reprinted through the kindness of the editors.

British Library Cataloguing in Publication Data

Trilling, Lionel
E. M. Forster. – (The works of Lionel Trilling)
1. Forster, E.M. – Criticism and interpretation
I. Title
823'.912   PR6011.058Z/
ISBN 0-19-212227-4

Printed in United States of America

To my Mother and Father

Preface to the Second Edition

THE PREFACE to a new edition of this little book must take note of two things that have happened since its original publication. The first is that Mr. Forster has added to the canon of his work as it existed when I wrote about it. In 1951 he brought out *Two Cheers for Democracy,* a collection of his literary and miscellaneous essays written since *Abinger Harvest;* in 1953 he gave us *The Hill of Devi,* a memoir of the Indian sojourn of his youth, and in 1956 *Marianne Thornton,* a biography of his great-aunt which is in effect a history of his family. The second occurrence is that in the intervening years a quite formidable body of criticism has grown up around Mr. Forster's novels. When I wrote my study, Mr. Forster was already a cherished author, and his work had called forth, especially in England, a critical literature of some size. Since that time, Mr. Forster's work has become ever more widely known, and, we may say, known in a new, a more public, way—where once it had been admired by many who found pleasure in thinking that it was known to them alone, a private experience to be kindly but cautiously shared with a few others of like mind, it has now become a general possession, securely established in the literary tradition of our time, and something like required reading for educated people. The growth of Mr. Forster's fame is being matched, expectably enough, by the increase of the critical attention that is paid him. This development is especially marked in America, where he is now one of the approved subjects for the university scholar of literature.

No doubt this work of mine would have the appearance of being more nearly complete if I were now to bring into its purview Mr. Forster's three latest books and take into account the augmented corpus of criticism. But when I consider the nature and purpose of my study, I am not able to convince myself that by this revision I should be contributing to much more than an appearance. Of the essays that are gathered together in *Two Cheers for Democracy,* some were available to me upon their first publication; those that appeared after I wrote are valuable indeed, but they do not lead me to revise my description of the temper of Mr. Forster's mind when he speaks in his own person as a critic of literature and society. *The Hill of Devi* and *Marianne Thornton* do certainly deepen our awareness of Mr. Forster as a personality and a "figure" in our culture, and of course I had not failed—could scarcely have failed—to respond to him in that aspect. But even though this interest was strong, it was ancillary to my primary concern, which was with the author of the novels, and although the two delightful new books do in a sense bear upon Mr. Forster's art, for they suggest some of the personal circumstances which the novelist used as "material," yet neither of them has worked any essential change in the view of the novelist which I had set forth before they appeared.

When I began my study, I naturally made myself aware of the critical climate in which Mr. Forster's work then existed, but it was far from my purpose to take particular account of it, and it does not seem appropriate that I should now revise my old intention. Of the critical writings that have appeared in the intervening time, some disagree with what I said, and many go beyond me in complexity or ingenuity of perception and interpretation. I could only seem contentious if I were to attempt to deal with the differences of opinion. And although I do indeed recognize that some new readings of the novels are more developed than mine, I suppose that the close student of Forster will wish to consult all the opinions, the old and the new, at first hand. As for the beginning reader of Forster, he could only be burdened and confused by an account of the multiplicity of views, and, indeed, for him there may even be some advantage in my by now primitive simplicity.

Preface to the Second Edition

For this edition, then, I have expanded the bibliography to apprise the reader of what he may want to consult in the way of critical opinion beyond my own book. I have corrected a few literal or factual errors in the text but have made no other changes in it.

I should add that even if I had convinced myself that revision was necessary, I would probably have had to decide that it was neither possible nor right for me to undertake it. Most of the book was written, as I well remember, in a concentrated rush, and although much of the enthusiasm and pleasure of its composition is to be attributed to my liking for the subject, I have no doubt that I was benefited by the special energies that attend a polemical purpose. To some readers it will perhaps seem strange, even perverse, to have involved Mr. Forster in polemic, but I did just that—I had a quarrel with American literature as at that time it was established, and against what seemed to me its dullness and its pious social simplicities I enlisted Mr. Forster's vivacity, complexity, and irony. It was a quarrel that was to occupy me for some years; from the title of the introductory chapter of this book I took the name of my first volume of essays, *The Liberal Imagination*. The occasion of that cultural contention no longer exists, at least not in its old form, but it was an event of some importance in my intellectual life and I would not wish to interfere with what I said in the course of it. I feel this the more for a reason which is not personal—the old quarrel, which of course I did not engage in alone, is part of our literary history, and even the smallest historical document ought not to be tampered with.

One other circumstance would stand in the way of revision. When I wrote the book, I was not acquainted with Mr. Forster and there was no communication between us. Since then we have become—I hope Mr. Forster will allow me to say—friends. Friendship, I am sure, does not necessarily make disinterested criticism impossible, but sometimes makes it difficult; and perhaps this is most likely when the critic sees a very close consonance between the author and his work. I find that when I now think of the novels, certain affectionate recollections of Mr. Forster himself intrude upon my judgment. I have no wish to drive them away, but I think that the reader, and Mr. Forster's art, and criticism itself, are best served by my early and impersonal opinions.

L.T.

New York
1964

Contents

E. M. Forster

CHAPTER ONE

Introduction: Forster and the Liberal Imagination

E. M. FORSTER is for me the only living novelist who can be read again and again and who, after each reading, gives me what few writers can give us after our first days of novel-reading, the sensation of having learned something. I have wanted for a long time to write about him and it gives me a special satisfaction to write about him now, for a consideration of Forster's work is, I think, useful in time of war.

In America Forster has never established a great reputation. Perhaps his readers are more numerous than I suppose, but at best they make a quiet band, and his novels—excepting *A Passage to India,* and that for possibly fortuitous reasons—are still esoteric with us. In England, although scarcely a popular writer, he is widely known and highly regarded; still, it is not at all certain whether even in England he is properly regarded and truly known. Some of the younger writers—among them Christopher Isherwood and Cyril Connolly—hold him in great esteem and have written well about him; I. A. Richards' remarks about Forster are sometimes perceptive, Elizabeth Bowen has spoken of him briefly but well, and the late Peter Burra's essay (now the introduction to the Everyman edition of *A Passage to India*) is a sound appreciation. But both Rose Macaulay and Virginia Woolf, who write of Forster with admiration, perceive the delicacy but not the cogency of his mind. As for the judgment canonized in *The Concise Cambridge History of English Literature,* it is wholly mistaken; the "shy, unworldly quality" of work "almost diffidently presented" by a man who is "at heart a scholar" simply does not exist. The author of this comment has taken an irony literally and has misinterpreted a manner.

It is Forster's manner, no doubt, that prevents a greater response to his work. That manner is comic; Forster owes much to Fielding, Dickens, Meredith and James. And nowadays even the literate reader is likely to be unschooled in the comic tradition and unaware of the comic seriousness. The distinction between the serious and the solemn is an old one, but it must be made here again to explain one of the few truly serious novelists of our time. Stendhal believed that gaiety was one of the marks of the healthy intelligence, and we are mistakenly sure that Stendhal was wrong. We suppose that there is necessarily an intellectual "depth" in the deep tones of the organ; it is possibly the sign of a deprivation—our suspicion of gaiety in art perhaps signifies an inadequate seriousness in ourselves. A generation charmed by the lugubrious—once in O'Neill, Dreiser and Anderson, now in Steinbeck and Van Wyck Brooks—is perhaps fleeing from the trivial shape of its own thoughts.

Forster is not only comic, he is often playful. He is sometimes irritating in his refusal to be great. Greatness in literature, even in comedy, seems to have some affinity with greatness in government and war, suggesting power, a certain sternness, a touch of the imperial and imperious. But Forster, who in certain moods might say with Swift, "I have hated all nations, professions and communities, and all my love is for individuals," fears power and suspects formality as the sign of power. "Distrust every enterprise that requires new clothes" is the motto one of his characters inscribes over his wardrobe. It is a maxim of only limited wisdom; new thoughts sometimes need new clothes and the seriousness of Forster's intellectual enterprise is too often reduced by the unbuttoned manner he affects. The quaint, the facetious and the chatty sink his literary criticism below its proper level; they diminish the stature of his short fiction and they even touch, though they never actually harm, the five novels; the true comic note sometimes drops to mere chaff and we now and then wish that the style were less comfortable and more arrogant.

But while these lapses have to be reckoned with, they do not negate the validity of the manner of which they are the deficiency or excess. Forster's manner is the agent of a moral intention which can only be carried out by the mind *ondoyant et divers* of which Montaigne spoke. What Forster wants to know about the human heart must be caught by surprise, by what he calls the "relaxed will," and if not everything can be caught in this way, what is so caught cannot be caught in any other way. Rigor will not do, and Forster uses the novel as a form amenable to the most arbitrary manipulation. He teases his medium and plays with his genre. He scorns the fetish of "adequate motivation," delights in surprise and melodrama and has a kind of addiction to sudden death. Guiding his stories according to his serious whim—like the anonymous lady, he has a whim of iron—Forster takes full and conscious responsibility for his novels, refusing to share in the increasingly dull assumption of the contemporary novelist, that the writer has nothing to do with the story he tells and that, *mirabile dictu,* through no intention of his own, the story has chosen to tell itself through him. Like Fielding, he shapes his prose for comment and explanation, and like Fielding he is not above an explanatory footnote. He summarizes what he is going to show, introduces new themes when and as it suits him to do so, is not awed by the sacred doctrine of "point of view" and, understanding that verisimilitude, which more than one critic has defended from his indifference, can guarantee neither pleasure nor truth, he uses exaggeration and improbability. As a result, the four novels up to *A Passage to India* all suggest that they have been written after a close application to the dramatic principles of *The Winter's Tale.*

In all this Forster is not bizarre. He simply has the certainty of the great novelists that any novel is a made-up thing and that a story, in order to stand firmly on reality, needs to keep no more than one foot on probability. Against this belief is opposed our increasingly grim realistic prejudice: we have learned to believe that *The Winter's Tale* is great poetry but bad dramaturgy. Our literal and liberal intelligence jibs at an interruption of sixteen years, at what we are convinced is an improbability not only of event but of emotion—we think it wrong that Mamillius and Antigonus should die so casually, or that anyone should "exit, pursued by a bear," or that Polixenes should fly into his brutal rage after having so charmingly taken part in Perdita's great flower scene, for it confuses us that good and evil should coexist and alternate. To accept Forster we have to know that *The Winter's Tale* is dramatically and morally sound and that improbability is the guide to life.

This means an affirmation of faith in the masters of the novel, in James, Meredith, Dickens—and in Hawthorne, whose notion of the "romance" (for he was forced to distinguish his own kind of novel from the more literal kind) is here so suggestive.

When a writer calls his work a Romance, it need hardly be observed that he wishes to claim a certain latitude, both as to its fashion and material, which he would not have felt himself entitled to assume had he professed to be writing a Novel. The latter form of composition is presumed to aim at a very minute fidelity, not merely to the possible, but to the probable and ordinary course of man's experience. The former—while, as a work of art, it must rigidly subject itself to laws, and while it sins unpardonably so far as it may swerve aside from the truth of the human heart—has fairly a right to present that truth under circumstances, to a great extent, of the writer's own choosing or creation.

Hawthorne is no doubt the greater artist and perhaps the greater moralist, yet Forster stands with him in his unremitting concern with moral realism. All novelists deal with morality, but not all novelists, or even all good novelists, are concerned with moral realism, which is not the awareness of morality itself but of the contradictions, paradoxes and dangers of living the moral life. To the understanding of the inextricable tangle of good and evil and of how perilous moral action can be, Hawthorne was entirely devoted. Henry James followed him in this devotion and after James, though in a smaller way, comes Forster, who can say of one of his characters that he was "cursed with the Primal Curse, which is not the knowledge of good and evil, but the knowledge of good-and-evil."

It is here that the precise point of Forster's manner appears. Forster's plots are always sharp and definite, for he expresses difference by means of struggle, and struggle by means of open conflict so intense as to flare into melodrama and even into physical violence. Across each of his novels runs a barricade; the opposed forces on each side are Good and Evil in the forms of Life and Death, Light and Darkness, Fertility and Sterility, Courage and Respectability, Intelligence and Stupidity—all the great absolutes that are so dull when discussed in themselves. The comic manner, however, will not tolerate absolutes. It stands on the barricade and casts doubt on both sides. The fierce plots move forward to grand simplicities but the comic manner confuses the issues, forcing upon us the difficulties and complications of the moral fact. The plot suggests eternal division, the manner reconciliation; the plot speaks of clear certainties, the manner resolutely insists that nothing can be quite so simple. "Wash ye, make yourselves clean," says the plot, and the manner murmurs, "If you can find the soap."

Now, to the simple mind the mention of complication looks like a kind of malice, and to the mind under great stress the suggestion of something "behind" the apparent fact looks like a call to quietism, like mere shilly-shallying. And this is the judgment, I think, that a great many readers of the most enlightened sort are likely to pass on Forster. For he stands in a peculiar reaction to what, for want of a better word, we may call the liberal tradition, that loose body of middle-class opinion which includes such ideas as progress, collectivism and humanitarianism.

To this tradition Forster has long been committed—all his novels are politically and morally tendentious and always in the liberal direction. Yet he is deeply at odds with the liberal mind, and while liberal readers can go a long way with Forster, they can seldom go all the way. They can understand him when he attacks the manners and morals of the British middle class, when he speaks out for spontaneity of feeling, for the virtues of sexual fulfillment, for the values of intelligence; they go along with him when he speaks against the class system, satirizes soldiers and officials, questions the British Empire and attacks business ethics and the public schools. But sooner or later they begin to make reservations and draw back. They suspect Forster is not quite playing their game; they feel that he is challenging *them* as well as what they dislike. And they are right. For all his long commitment to the doctrines of liberalism, Forster is at war with the liberal imagination.

Surely if liberalism has a single desperate weakness, it is an inadequacy of imagination: liberalism is always being surprised. There is always the liberal work to do over again because disillusionment and fatigue follow hard upon surprise, and reaction is always ready for that moment of liberal disillusionment and fatigue—reaction never hopes, despairs or suffers amazement. Liberalism likes to suggest its affinity with science, pragmatism and the method of hypothesis, but in actual conduct it requires "ideals" and absolutes; it prefers to make its alliances only when it thinks it catches the scent of Utopia in parties and governments, the odor of sanctity in men; and if neither is actually present, liberalism makes sure to supply it. When liberalism must act with some degree of anomaly—and much necessary action is anomalous—it insists that it is acting on perfect theory and is astonished when anomaly then appears.

The liberal mind is sure that the order of human affairs owes it a simple logic: good is good and bad is bad. It can understand, for it invented and named, the moods of optimism and pessimism, but the mood that is the response to good-and-evil it has not named and cannot understand. Before the idea of good-and-evil its imagination fails; it cannot accept this improbable paradox. This is ironic, for one of the charter-documents of liberalism urges the liberal mind to cultivate imagination enough to accept just this improbability.

Good and evil we know in the field of this world grow up together almost inseparably; and the knowledge of good is so involved and interwoven with the knowledge of evil, and in so many cunning resemblances hardly to be discerned, that those confused seeds which were imposed upon Psyche as an incessant labor to cull out, and sort asunder, were not more intermixed. It was from out the rind of one apple tasted, that the knowledge of good and evil, as two twins cleaving together, leaped forth into the world. And perhaps this is that doom which Adam fell into of knowing good and evil, that is to say of knowing good by evil.

And the irony is doubled when we think how well the great conservative minds have understood what Milton meant. Dr. Johnson and Burke and, in a lesser way at a later time, Fitzjames Stephen, understood the mystery of the twins; and Matthew Arnold has always been thought the less a liberal for his understanding of them. But we of the liberal connection have always liked to play the old intellectual game of antagonistic principles. It is an attractive game because it gives us the sensation of thinking, and its first rule is that if one of two opposed principles is wrong, the other is necessarily right. Forster will not play this game; or, rather, he plays it only to mock it.

This indifference to the commonplaces of liberal thought makes the very texture of Forster's novels and appeared in the first of them. The theme of *Where Angels Fear to Tread* is the violent opposition between British respectability and a kind of pagan and masculine integration. D. H. Lawrence, who played the old game of antagonistic principles for all it was worth—and it was worth something in his hands—gave us many characters like Forster's Gino Carella, characters who, like Gino, were cruel (the scene of Gino's cruelty is, incidentally, one of the most remarkable in modern fiction) or, like Gino, indifferent to the "higher" and romantic emotions. But here Lawrence always stopped; from this point on all his effort went to intensifying his picture, and by this he no doubt gained, as against Forster, in sheer coercive power. For the poor, lost, respectable British people, Gino may serve as the embodiment of the masculine and pagan principle, but Forster knows that he is also coarse, dull, vain, pretentious, facilely polite and very much taken with the charms of respectability.

And it is irritating to be promised a principle and then to be given only an hypothesis. The hypothesis, having led us to criticize respectability, is useful, but we had wanted it to be conclusive. And

Forster refuses to be conclusive. No sooner does he come to a conclusion than he must unravel it again. In *A Room with a View,* to
take another example, he leads us to make the typical liberal discovery that Miss Bartlett, the poor relation who thinks she is acting
from duty, is really acting from a kind of malice—she has been
trying to recruit the unawakened heroine into "the armies of the benighted, who follow neither the heart nor the brain." But Forster
does not stop at this conventionality, even though in 1908 it was not
quite so conventional. For when the heroine at last fulfills her destiny, deserts Miss Bartlett and marries the man she had unconsciously loved (this is, to all appearance, a very modest little novel),
she comes to perceive that in some yet more hidden way Miss
Bartlett had really desired the union. And we have been prepared
for this demonstration of the something still further "behind" the
apparent by the action of the tolerant and enlightened clergyman,
Mr. Beebe, who has ceased to be the angel of light and has set
himself against the betrothal.

Forster's insistence on the double turn, on the something else that
lies behind, is sometimes taken for "tolerance," but although it often
suggests forgiveness (a different thing), it almost as often makes
the severest judgments. And even when it suggests forgiveness it
does not spring so much from gentleness of heart as from respect
for two facts coexisting, from the moral realism that understands
the one apple tasted. Forster can despise Gerald of *The Longest
Journey* because Gerald is a prig and a bully, but he can invest
Gerald's death with a kind of primitive dignity, telling us of the
maid-servants who weep, "They had not liked Gerald, but he was a
man, they were women, he had died." And after Gerald's death he
can give Agnes Pembroke her moment of tragic nobility, only to
pursue her implacably for her genteel brutality.

So much moral realism is rare enough to be a kind of surprise,
and Forster, as I have said, likes to work with surprises mild or
great. "Gerald died that afternoon," is the beginning of a chapter
which follows immediately upon a description of Gerald full of
superabundant life. We have to stand unusually far back from For-

ster's characters not to be startled when they turn about, and the peculiar pleasure to be had from his books is that of a judicious imperturbability. He is always shocking us by removing the heroism of his heroes and heroines; in *A Passage to India,* Mrs. Moore, of whom we had expected high actions, lets herself be sent away from the trial at which her testimony would have been crucial; Cyril Fielding, who as a solitary man had heroically opposed official ideas, himself becomes official when he is successful and married; and Dr. Aziz cannot keep to his role of the sensitive and enlightened native. It is a tampering with the heroic in the manner not of Lytton Strachey but of Tolstoy, a kind of mithridate against our being surprised by life. Let us not deceive ourselves, Forster seems to say, it is with just such frailties as Mrs. Moore and Mr. Fielding, and with and for such unregeneracies as Dr. Aziz that the problem of, let us say, India must be solved. The moments of any man's apparent grace are few, any man may have them and their effects are not easily to be calculated. It is on a helter-skelter distribution of grace that Forster pins what hopes he has; but for years after *A Passage to India*—it is still his latest novel—he has had the increasing sense of possible doom.

Perhaps it is because he has nothing of the taste for the unconditioned—Nietzsche calls it the worst of all tastes, the taste that is always being fooled by the world—that Forster has been able to deal so well with the idea of class. The liberal mind has in our time spoken much of this idea but has failed to believe in it. The modern liberal believes in categories and wage-scales and calls these class. Forster knows better, and in *Howards End* shows the conflicting truths of the idea—that on the one hand class is character, soul and destiny, and that on the other hand class is not finally determining. He knows that class may be truly represented only by struggle and contradiction, not by description, and preferably by moral struggle in the heart of a single person. When D. H. Lawrence wrote to Forster that he had made "a nearly deadly mistake glorifying those *business* people in *Howards End.* Business is no good," he was indulging his own taste for the unconditioned. It led him to read

Forster inaccurately and it led him to make that significant shift from "business people" to "business." But Forster, who is too worldly to suppose that we can judge people without reference to their class, is also too worldly to suppose that we can judge class-conditioned action until we make a hypothetical deduction of the subject's essential humanity. It is exactly because Forster can judge the "business people" as he does, and because he can judge the lower classes so without sentimentality, that he can deal firmly and intelligently with his own class, and if there is muddle in *Howards End*—and the nearly allegorical reconciliation is rather forced—then, in speaking of class, clear ideas are perhaps a sign of ignorance, muddle the sign of true knowledge; surely *Howards End* stands with *Our Mutual Friend* and *The Princess Casamassima* as one of the great comments on the class struggle.

To an American, one of the most notable things about Forster's work is the directness and consciousness of its connection with tradition. We know of Forster that he is a Hellenist but not a "classicist," that he loves Greece in its mythical and naturalistic aspects, that Plato has never meant much to him, perhaps because he mistrusts the Platonic drive to the absolute and the Platonic judgment of the body and the senses. He dislikes the Middle Ages and all in Dante that is medieval. He speaks of himself as a humanist and traces his descent to Erasmus and Montaigne. He is clearly in the romantic line, yet his admiration for Goethe and Shelley is qualified; Beethoven is a passion with him but he distrusts Schumann. He has no faith in the regenerative power of Christianity and he is frequently hostile to the clergy, yet he has a tenderness for religion because it expresses, though it does not solve, the human mystery; in this connection it is worth recalling that he once projected a book on Samuel Butler. I list these preferences of Forster's not because I wish to bound his intellectual life—so brief a list could not do that—but because enumerating them will help to suggest how hard it would be to name an American novelist whose connection with intellectual tradition is equally clear. In America the opinion still prevails, though not so strongly as it once did, that a conscious relation with the past can only debilitate a novelist's powers, dull his perceptions and prevent his experience of life.

Yet if we test the matter we must come to a contrary conclusion. Sherwood Anderson, for example, though at first it may seem strange to say so, had much in common with Forster. The original gifts of the two men, so far as we can measure such things, might for purposes of argument be judged nearly equal. Each set himself in opposition to the respectable middle class of his own country and each found a symbolic contrast in an alien and, as it seemed, a freer race. Each celebrated the salvation of the loving heart, the passionate body and the liberated personality. Yet as Anderson went on, he grew more and more out of touch with the life he represented and criticized, and it was as if, however much he might experience beyond a certain point, he had not the means to receive and order what he felt, and so ceased really to feel. In his later years he became, as gifted men of a certain temperament tend to become, symbolic and visionary, but, never understanding how to handle his ultimate hopes and his obscurer insights, he began to repeat himself and become increasingly vague. The vision itself began to fail when Anderson could not properly judge its importance and could not find for it the right symbols and the right language; and in his later years he made the impression, terribly touching, of being lost and alone.

He was indeed lost and alone, though he need not have been. But the men with whom he might have made community were not to be found where he thought they were, in the stable and the crafts-man's shop. The men of Anderson's true community were the members of the European tradition of thought. But Anderson was either indifferent to the past or professionally contemptuous of it; he subscribed to the belief that American art must throw off the shackles of tradition and work only with intuition and observation. Anderson saw "culture" as gentility; and he saw it too, one feels, as a kind of homogeneous mass to be accepted or rejected only in totality; he did not know that it was a collection of individuals much like himself with whom he might claim kinship and equality, nor did he know that what he was demanding for life had been demanded by other men time out of mind. Anderson's books, like so many other American books, had at first a great and taking power; then, like so many other American books that have astonished and delighted us, they fell out of the texture of our lives, they became curiosities.

Let us say the worst we can of Forster—that beside a man like Anderson with his tumble of emotions and child-like questions, Forster might seem to have something donnish about him. But then we must at once say that Forster has a sense of the way things go which Anderson, for all his great explicit impulse toward actuality, never had—the sense of what houses, classes, institutions, politics, manners and people are like. Forster knows, as Anderson never knew, that things are really there. All his training has helped bring his impulses to consciousness, and the play of consciousness over intuition and desire gives him his curious tough insight.

The great thing Forster has been able to learn from his attachment to tradition and from his sense of the past is his belief in the present. He has learned not to be what most of us are—eschatological. Most of us, consciously or unconsciously, are discontented with the nature rather than with the use of the human faculty; deep in our assumption lies the hope and the belief that humanity will end its career by developing virtues which will be admirable exactly because we cannot now conceive them. The past has been a weary failure, the present cannot matter, for it is but a step forward to the final judgment; we look to the future when the best of the works of man will seem but the futile and slightly disgusting twitchings of primeval creatures: thus, in the name of a superior and contemptuous posterity, we express our self-hatred—and our desire for power.

This is a moral and historical error into which Forster never falls; his whole work, indeed, is an implied protest against it. The very relaxation of his style, its colloquial unpretentiousness, is a mark of his acceptance of the human fact as we know it now. He is content with the human possibility and content with its limitations. The way of human action of course does not satisfy him, but he does not believe there are any new virtues to be discovered; not by becoming better, he says, but by ordering and distributing his native goodness can man live as befits him.

This, it seems to me, might well be called worldliness, this acceptance of man in the world without the sentimentality of cynicism and without the sentimentality of rationalism. Forster is that remarkably rare being, a naturalist whose naturalism is positive and passionate, not negative, passive and apologetic for man's nature. He accepts the many things the liberal imagination likes to put out of sight. He can accept, for example, not only the reality but the power of death—"Death destroys a man, but the idea of death saves him," he says, and the fine scene in *The Longest Journey* in which Rickie forces Agnes to "mind" the death of Gerald is a criticism not only of the British fear of emotion but also of liberalism's incompetence before tragedy. To Forster, as to Blake, naturalism suggests not the invalidity or the irrelevance of human emotions but, rather, their validity and strength: "Far more mysterious than the call of sex to sex is the tenderness that we throw into that call; far wider is the gulf between us and the farmyard than between the farmyard and the garbage that nourishes it."

He is so worldly, indeed, that he believes that ideas are for his service and not for his worship. In 1939 when war was certain and the talk ran so high and loose about Democracy that it was hard to know what was being talked about, Forster remarked with the easy simplicity of a man in his own house, "So two cheers for Democracy; one because it admits variety and two because it permits criticism. Two cheers are quite enough: there is no occasion to give three. Only Love the Beloved Republic deserves that." He is so worldly that he has always felt that his nation belonged to him. He has always known that we cannot love anything bigger until we first love what Burke called "the little platoon" and so it has been easy for him to speak of his love for his country with whose faults he has never ceased to quarrel; and now he has no void to fill up with that acrid nationalism that literary men too often feel called upon to express in a time of crisis. He is one of the thinking people who were never led by thought to suppose they could be more than human and who, in bad times, will not become less.

CHAPTER TWO

Sawston and Cambridge

EDWARD MORGAN FORSTER was born on January 1, 1879. The place of his birth and the origin and position of his family have at least a symbolic bearing on his development. The place was London and, although Forster has been anything but a lover of the city, his culture, with its accessibility to new ideas, is essentially metropolitan. His father, an architect, was on the paternal side of Anglo-Irish extraction and through his mother was descended from a family which for some generations had been notable members of the intellectual middle class—originally, indeed, of the Clapham Sect of wealthy Evangelicals. In his essay, "Battersea Rise," [1] Forster speaks of his great-grandfather's London house in whose library William Wilberforce, James Stephen, Zachary Macaulay, Thomas Babington and, sometimes, Hannah More met to transact their religious and philanthropic business. Very sensitive to the evils of the slave trade which they were instrumental in abolishing, quite impervious to the evils of the manufacturing system, these were people who lived by public spirit and by ideas, however narrow. [2] Forster was to attack much of what they stood for, but he had

[1] In *Abinger Harvest*. Unless otherwise noted, all the essays to which I refer are included in this volume.

[2] In an essay in *The New Statesman and Nation* (April 1, 1939), Forster writes at some length of Henry Thornton, his great-grandfather, and speaks of his two very successful books. One was a volume of family prayers, posthumously collected, which

been born in the intellectual citadel of a solid and powerful class and he drew strength and confidence from it. He undertook with peculiar ease at an early age the profession of the intellectual life, and in his latter age, in a time when intellectuals are not in good repute even with themselves, he continues to be unwearied of his profession and to justify it.

The young Forster was schooled at Tonbridge, which figures as the "Sawston" of his two first novels. In *Where Angels Fear to Tread* the town of Sawston stands as the stronghold of genteel, snobbish philistinism, the source of all illusion, and in *The Longest Journey* Sawston School plays a large and dreadful part. The latter novel is at least obliquely autobiographical[3] and testifies to the unhappiness of Forster's school days. He was a day-boy, a fact which he finds significant enough to include in the biographical note of ten short lines which appears in the Everyman edition of *A Passage to India*. The position of day-boys in boarding schools is traditionally bad and *The Longest Journey* records almost passionately the snubbing they received at Sawston.

But even had he not been at a disadvantage, it is unlikely that Forster would have been happy at his public school. Few gifted boys have been, and the literary men of our time continue the indictments which have made the English public schools a matter of controversy and even of political conflict since early in the 19th century. G. Lowes Dickinson was equally unhappy at Charterhouse and Forster, in a biography of this friend, is clearly drawing upon his own experience when he describes Dickinson's surprised relief upon discovering "that the public school is not infinite and eternal, that there is something more compelling in life than team work and

---

"between 1834 and 1854 . . . ran into as many as thirty-one editions." The other was a work on banking, *Essay On Paper Credit*, still regarded as sufficiently useful to be recently republished in an edition by Professor F. A. von Hayek (Allen and Unwin). Between them, the two books, as Forster implies, neatly comprehend the nature of Clapman Evangelicism.

[3] The history of Sawston School in Chapter IV follows very closely the actual history of Tonbridge School.

more vital than cricket, that firmness and self-complacency do not between them compose the whole armour of man."

Sawston-Tonbridge may have made Forster miserable but it gave his thought its great central theme. This is the theme of the undeveloped heart. In his essay, "Notes on the English Character," Forster speaks of the public school system as being at the root of England's worst national faults and most grievous political errors. For, he says, the faults of England are the faults of the middle classes that dominate it, and the very core of these middle classes is the English public school system, which gives its young men a weight out of all proportion to their numbers and sends them into a world "of whose richness and subtlety they have no conception," a world into which they go "with well-developed bodies, fairly developed minds and undeveloped hearts."

The theme is almost obsessive with Forster. It is not the unfeeling or perverted heart that absorbs him, but the heart untrained and untutored, the heart checked too early in its natural possible growth. His whole literary effort is a research into this profound pathology.

And if Forster's public school presented him with his dominant theme, his university taught him how to deal with it. What Cambridge gave Forster was, in his own judgment, invaluable; *The Longest Journey* and the biography of Lowes Dickinson record his gratitude.

The tutors and resident fellows . . . treated with rare dexterity the products that came up yearly from the public schools. They taught the perky boy that he was not everything, and the limp boy that he might be something. They even welcomed those boys who were neither limp nor perky, but odd—those boys who had never been at a public school at all, and such do not find a welcome everywhere. And they did everything with ease—one might almost say with nonchalance—so that boys noticed nothing and received education, often for the first time in their lives.

It is a fine compliment for a university to receive, although perhaps the one Forster puts into the mouth of young Stewart Ansell is even finer.

"The good societies say, 'I tell you to do that because I am Cambridge.' The bad ones say, 'I tell you to do that because I am the great world'— not because I am 'Peckham' or 'Billingsgate' or 'Park Lane,' but 'because I am the great world.' They lie."

Cambridge did not lie to Forster, did not claim too much, and therefore did its work well. It was the perfect antithesis to Sawston-Tonbridge exactly because it resolved for him, as for Dickinson before him, all the false antitheses the public school had contrived.

Body and spirit, reason and emotion, work and play, architecture and scenery, laughter and seriousness, life and art—these pairs which are elsewhere contrasted were there fused into one. People and books reinforced one another, intelligence joined hands with affection, speculation became a passion, and discussion was made profound by love.

Dickinson, seventeen years older than Forster, was a Fellow of King's when Forster entered that college in the autumn of 1897. The two were to become close friends and Dickinson's influence was eventually to be considerable, but their relationship began late and was never the formal one of student and teacher. Forster took a classical degree in 1900[4] and when, in his fourth year, he turned from classics to history, intending to do his essay work with Dickinson, he was cajoled by Oscar Browning into coming to him instead.

Browning, the legendary "O.B.," has been called (by E. F. Benson) "a genius flawed by abysmal fatuity." Hugely fat (he could not tie his own shoes), monumentally and comically snobbish, alternately brilliant and silly, he had a passion for educating young men, and Forster, while testifying to the erroneousness of Browning's information and to the intolerable way he conveyed it, testifies also to his talent for teaching. Forster himself came toward the end of Browning's glory and was not much influenced by him, but his existence in King's suggests something of the liveliness of the college. The decisive influence on Forster was his classics tutor, Nathaniel Wedd, a cynical, aggressive, Mephistophelean character who affected red

---

[4] The official details of Forster's Cambridge career include his being an Exhibitioner, a Prizeman, his taking a Second Class in the Classical Tripos, Part I, in 1900, and a Second Class in the Historical Tripos, Part II, in 1901. He took his M.A. in 1910; he was elected Fellow of his College in 1927.

ties and blasphemy. "It is to him rather than to Dickinson—indeed to him more than to anyone—that I owe such awakening as has befallen me," Forster says in his biography of Dickinson. "It is through him that I can best imagine the honesty and fervour of fifty years back."

From Wedd Forster acquired much of that feeling for the classics and for Greece which, colored by Wedd's political and social ideas, was to be his chief instrument against Sawston. His Greece is his own Greece, or Wedd's Greece, or Cambridge's Greece—every Greece is different from every other, each being shaped for a particular purpose. Forster's is the Greece of myth and mystery, of open skies and athleticism, of love and democracy. It is not the "true" Greece, but no Greece is, and at least it is not the Greece of moral precept, not the Greece that, as Mr. Jackson says in *The Longest Journey*, produced an enlightened bishop named Sophocles and other poets who were Broad Church clergymen.

It was under the Cambridge influence of Wedd and Dickinson that Forster made his first and lasting political choice. In 1903 Wedd and Dickinson, together with a group that included the historian G. M. Trevelyan, founded *The Independent Review*. "The main aim of the review was political," Forster writes in the Dickinson biography. "It was founded to combat the aggressive Imperialism and Protection campaign of Joe Chamberlain; and to advocate sanity in foreign affairs and a constructive policy at home. It was not so much a Liberal Review as an appeal to Liberalism from the left to be its better self—one of those appeals which have continued until the extinction of the Liberal party." An appeal to the Liberal party —to the middle class—from the left was to be the mode of Forster's political action from this time on.

And with the founding of *The Independent Review* Forster took his first step into the literary life with a political élan that has continued to be an element of all his writing. When he bought the first issue of the *Independent*, he "thought the new age had begun." He was soon contributing to its pages.

Forster was twenty-four when his writing began to appear and he brought out his first novel at twenty-six. The quality of maturity which he exhibited is no doubt an evidence of his own powers, but it is also an evidence of the success Cambridge had had in educating him. According to the American myth, less powerful now than formerly, which assumes a mortal antagonism between the creative and the intellectual life, the university is a particularly deadly influence upon the creative mind. Of the dominant figures of American literature in the last forty years, most have not been university men, or, if they have, they have usually been indifferent to or scornful of their university careers. But in England forty-odd years ago, a student at Cambridge was not likely to suppose that the university of Marlowe, Milton, Dryden and Coleridge was going to desiccate him by scholarship or make him into a don when he wanted to be a poet. The security of this literary-academic connection must have meant much in Forster's development.

But perhaps even more important was the centrality to the national life which Cambridge shares with Oxford. No American university has a similar relation to its country. For one thing, the ancient English universities have a quasi-national foundation. Each elects a member to Parliament and both hold an institutional and traditional place in a nation which is more cohesive than ours. For England is not only smaller but more familial than America. Class no doubt makes great divisions and the English classes are more sharply marked off than our own, but the divisions of class are in some respects not so wide, and certainly not so various, as our own divisions of regions and sections. A young man who is a member of an institution so ancient and so central as Cambridge might well acquire the sense of a nation in whose life he can participate, about which he can generalize and to which he can address himself.

Forster's own sense of his nation is acute and it greatly influences his treatment of the theme of the undeveloped heart. "His concern is with the private life," says Virginia Woolf in her essay on Forster in *The Death of the Moth* and in substantiation she quotes one among the many sentences Forster has written about the claims of the private life. But Mrs. Woolf's statement suggests that the interest in the private life is cultivated at the expense of the public life, whereas the very opposite is so. Forster is always concerned with the private life in its public connection and in "Notes on the English Character" his comments on the undeveloped heart conclude with the statement that the undeveloped heart is largely responsible for England's political difficulties. The private life is self-justified, but the right private life is further justified by its effect upon public life: privacy for Forster is never a personal provincialism. Passionately as he is aware of the delicacies of the private life, he is as passionate in his investigation of the complex relation between public and private and he has brought every subtle criterion of personality to bear upon the gross difficulties of politics. He makes his private judgments under the aspect of the nation—or of all the nations. This constitutes his uniqueness and his intellectual heroism.

And if, as I have said, some large part of the credit for Forster's sense of connection between the public and the private must go to Cambridge, then also to Cambridge must go some part of the credit for his early-developed literary manner, which is largely the result of his sense of a familial relation with his country. Forster's style at its best—and that is in the novels—is the style of personal discourse, a middle style, easy and lucid. It presupposes a reader, and it is intended to set the reader at ease and to convince or persuade without bullying. At its best it is simple and direct, as in the passages I have quoted in this chapter. This is a style that flourishes more easily in England than in America. Nothing determines style like the writer's sense of his audience, and in America the audience is less easily "seen," the voice must travel farther and it becomes less intimate.

The flowering of social criticism in England in the 19th century must surely have resulted from the feeling that England, however deranged, could still be talked to. A similar feeling never really developed in America and it is significant that two of our most remarkable social critics, Henry Adams and Thorstein Veblen, wrote difficult and self-conscious (though often fine) prose out of an embarrassed relation with their audience. In our own day critics like

Mencken, Mumford, Waldo Frank and Van Wyck Brooks, diverse as they are in their faults of style, all write English as if they did not quite know whom they were talking to; but Shaw and Chesterton, idiosyncratic as they pretend to be, write in perfectly normal prose.

Cyril Connolly, in his *Enemies of Promise,* has written at some length of Forster's style, finding its chief virtue in its colloquialism —its use of everyday words and its ease of movement in short and relatively simple sentences. "Much of his art," says Mr. Connolly, "consists in the plainness of his writing, for he is certain of the truth of his convictions and the force of his emotions. It is the writer who is not sure what to say or what he feels who is apt to overwrite either to conceal his ignorance or to come unexpectedly on an answer. Similarly it is the novelists who find it hard to create character who indulge in fine writing." This is true, yet so much emphasis on the plainness of Forster's diction must not keep from sight what is equally remarkable, the striking felicity of his style, its wit, its daring and its intensity. His prose with its notable happiness of expression is not merely an atmosphere of his novels—it is, indeed, one of the characters. Nor should a proper sense of its plainness obscure the eloquence—one should not, out of respect for prose, call it "poetry"— to which it can rise. Sometimes this eloquence can quite overstep itself and become merely "fine"—I. A. Richards is justified when he catches in Forster a tendency to "put it over" with eloquent pathos: the last pages of *The Longest Journey* are a case in point. But most of Forster's eloquence succeeds wholly, as subsequent quotation will show. And if Forster's style is, as Mr. Connolly says, "even and unemphatic," it is far from being reticent; it speaks out, it calls things by their names: indeed, although his ability to express the emotions and to admire and praise them may ring strange on contemporary ears, it is one of Forster's most characteristic virtues.[5]

[5] Mr. Connolly finds Forster the innovator of the diction used by Virginia Woolf, Katherine Mansfield, David Garnett and Elizabeth Bowen, a statement which is not at variance with his previous remark that one of the reasons why Forster's work still remains fresh is that "his style has not been imitated." For Mr. Connolly, Forster's style constitutes "a revolutionary break from the Mandarin style" of James, Meredith, Conrad and Pater, but it seems to me that in its vivacity it has more likeness to "Mandarin" than to the prose manner of current "intelligent" novels.

The faults of Forster's style I have already touched upon. Some-times its relaxation goes too far, invites too much, becomes arch, whimsical and feminine, although these are faults that can be quite as exasperating in a woman writer (in Virginia Woolf as essayist, for example) as in a man. The faults appear later than the virtues, though they are latent from the first, and they inhere in certain essays of which admirers of Forster will say that they could not have been written by a lesser man but that they should not have been written by Forster.

In 1901, after a fourth year at Cambridge, Forster visited Greece and lived in Italy, returning to England in 1902. The Mediterranean world captured his young imagination as the Oriental world cap-tured his mature years; his early essays and tales are suffused with the ancient sunlight, and his first published story, "Albergo Empe-docle,"[6] tells of a dull young Englishman who finds on a visit to Acragas that in a former incarnation he had been an inhabitant of the town.

In Italy it was the Renaissance that spoke to Forster, in Greece it was some vaguely ancient pagan time. He joined the two in his essay on Gemistus Pletho, the Renaissance Greek who loved the pagan gods and did his part in the revival of Greek learning in Italy.[7] Touching at Cnidus, the young Forster's thoughts are of Demeter, "who alone among gods has true immortality."

The others continue, perchance, their existence, but are forgotten, be-cause the time came when they could not be loved. But to her, all over the world, rise prayers of idolatry from suffering men as well as suffering women, for she has transcended sex. And Poets too, generation after gen-eration, have sung in passionate incompetence of the hundred-flowered Narcissus and the rape of Persephone, and the wanderings of the God-dess, and her gift to us of corn and tears; so that generations of critics, obeying also their need, have censured the poets for reviving the effete mythology of Greece, and urged them to themes of living interest which shall touch the heart of today.

[6] This story has not been reprinted. It appeared in *Temple Bar*, December, 1903.
[7] In *A Room with a View*, Forster will mock an Englishman who lives in Florence and who, in dilettante fashion, writes about Gemistus Pletho.

Harold, the hero of "Albergo Empedocle," says of his Greek existence, "I was better, I saw better, heard better, thought better." And he adds, "I loved very differently . . . Yes, I also loved better too." For Forster, the Greek world challenged modernity and it challenged Christianity, even in their best and tenderest sensibilities. The essay "Macolnia Shops" describes a little toilet box of ancient Grecian workmanship and speaks of the old morality, the old emotions, which were so simple and so sound.

Another [figure in the relief] has hastened back to the *Argo* and he is pouring water down the throat of a sick friend. But he has drunk himself first. That man is as many centuries from self-denial as he is from self-consciousness. . . .

Thus the motives go: the Praise of Water and the Praise of Friendship. The second is greater than the first; but it must needs come after it in place.

The ruffianism of the Renaissance was a different matter, but it too was a challenge to the modern world, and Forster writes of Cardan, the 16th-century physician, astrologer and mathematician, not because he was admirable but because he was passionate in life and in thought and because "those ghosts who are still clothed with passion or thought are profitable companions." As Greece was to stand for truth, Italy was to stand for passion, and with these two ideals and these two symbols, Forster returned to the England whose heart was the public school.

CHAPTER THREE

The Short Stories:
A Statement of Themes

SURELY the Greek myths made too deep an impression on Forster: of the twelve stories that have been reprinted in *The Celestial Omnibus* and *The Eternal Moment*,[1] only two, "The Road from Colonus," and "The Eternal Moment," are not in the genre of mythical fantasy and these two endure best. The others have, sometimes, wit or point or charm, one of them, "The Story of the Siren," has power, and all of them are "true" but none of them is wholly satisfying. The two non-fantastic stories, however, succeed entirely. And they are of particular interest because they contain in embryo the themes, symbols and ideas of Forster's five novels.

"The Road from Colonus" is about old age and death, but chiefly it is about modern life: it tells of a commonplace English Oedipus who does not die properly at his Colonus and who therefore loses the transfiguration he might have had. The elderly Mr. Lucas is a tourist in Greece, traveling by donkey with his daughter and a party. One day, riding ahead of his companions, he arrives at a tiny hamlet. In a scorching landscape the hamlet is a deeply shaded spot,

[1] *The Celestial Omnibus* (1911) contains "The Story of a Panic," "The Other Side of the Hedge," "The Celestial Omnibus," "Other Kingdom," "The Curate's Friend," and "The Road from Colonus"; *The Eternal Moment* (1928) contains "The Machine Stops," "The Point of It," "Mr. Andrews," "Co-Ordination," "The Story of the Siren," and "The Eternal Moment."

sheltered by great plane-trees. The greatest tree of all overhangs the primitive inn; it is hollow and from its roots gushes a spring of living water. The symbolic juxtaposition of hot rocks and flowing water we have encountered in *The Waste Land;* the sheltering plane-tree might recall Handel's great song in *Xerxes* and the scene in Herodotus which Handel was dramatizing. It is a votive tree and its hollow has been hung with tiny images of arms, legs, hearts and brains, "tokens of some recovery of strength or wisdom or love." To Mr. Lucas, who in this moment has "discovered not only Greece, but England and all the world and life, there seemed nothing ludicrous in the desire to hang within the tree another votive offering—a little model of an entire man." For he has stepped into the tree, the living spring is at his feet, and as he leans back into the huge hollow trunk his peace is so great that he is almost unconscious. He is aroused by a shock—"the shock of an arrival perhaps, for when he opened his eyes, something unimagined, indefinable, had passed over all things, and made them intelligible and good."

There was meaning in the stoop of the old woman over her work, and in the quick motions of the little pig, and in her diminishing globe of wool. A young man came singing over the streams on a mule, and there was beauty in his pose and sincerity in his greeting. The sun made no accidental patterns upon the spreading roots of the trees, and there was intention in the nodding clumps of asphodel, and in the music of the water.

Meaning, intention, no accidental pattern—and a little further on we are told of the *coherent* beauty Mr. Lucas saw: we perceive that here, continuing through a long century, is still the romantic quest. The romantic spirits from Wordsworth to Matthew Arnold had looked for coherence in nature's apparently "accidental pattern"; they did not want to believe in a dead or mechanical or merely neutral universe; they wanted to find what Mr. Lucas found, "meaning" and "intention." And the nearest they could come to finding them was when they felt, like Mr. Lucas, the sense of being a "whole man," an experience which seemed most often to come to them in the quiet contemplation of Nature or of the ancient, traditional life of humanity. They hoped to believe, and sometimes they could (Wordsworth more easily than Arnold) what Mr. Lucas now believed as he looked at the votive images in the tree, that "there was no such thing as the solitude of nature, for the sorrow and joys of humanity had pressed into the bosom of the tree." Arnold wrote of the man who has passed beyond the demands of the modern will:

Tears

Are in his eyes, and in his ears
The murmur of a thousand years:
Before him he sees Life unroll,
A placid and continuous whole;
That general Life, which does not cease,
Whose secret is not joy, but peace;
That Life, whose dumb wish is not miss'd
If birth proceeds, if things subsist;
The life of plants, and stones, and rain:
The Life he craves; if not in vain
Fate gave, what Chance shall not control
His sad lucidity of soul.

But Mr. Lucas's sad lucidity of soul is not to be in his own control. His party rides up and finds him standing in the tree; his daughter Ethel sees to it that he changes his wet boots and socks. His companions, like himself, are enchanted by the place but in a touristy way, and Ethel, to show her sensibility, announces that she must spend a week here. Mr. Lucas takes her seriously—it is his heart's desire, which he has not been able to utter. But then it comes time to go and Ethel shows herself to be a false Antigone: her intention of staying was only a way of speaking. For Mr. Lucas, however, it seems salvation to linger here with the simple people of the hamlet; he refuses to go, he will not budge. A strong young man of the party picks him up like a child and sets him on his mule.

We next see the Lucases in London. Ethel is to be married. Mr. Lucas has become petulant, nagging, self-centered. His hated sister is coming to keep house for him, he has not been able to sleep for the sound of the dogs, cats, singing, piano-playing and the gurgling of water in the drains. Life has become only an annoyance.

And as he and Ethel sit at breakfast the mail arrives, bringing a package of asphodel bulbs from Athens. Ethel, to test her modern Greek, begins to read the old Athenian newspapers in which the bulbs are wrapped. She reads of a disaster; in a great storm the plane-tree with the spring had fallen upon the little inn, killing all its occupants—and on the evening of the very day the Lucases had been there. But Mr. Lucas does not remember the place; he is planning a letter to his landlord, complaining of dogs, children, music and running water and he is not much interested, not even when Ethel speaks of his "marvelous deliverance."

Freud has written an interpretation of *King Lear* in which he connects the legends of the Three Caskets with the legends of the Three Sisters, and with the familiar triads of the Fates, Norms and Graces; in the course of his exposition he says that the leaden casket —the one the wise man chooses—is symbolic of death, and he points out how often in mythology the goddess of death and the goddess of love are identified with each other. It is a fine complication of ideas and if it does not "interpret" the play, it does indeed suggest an additional meaning. "Eternal wisdom in the garb of the primitive myth," Freud concludes, "bids the old man renounce love, choose death and make friends with dying"; but the love-goddess and the death-goddess are one, as Freud says, and are united in Cordelia. And in Forster's story death and love are one. "Death destroys a man," he says in *Howards End,* "but the idea of death saves him— that is the best account of it that has yet been given." In the same novel Helen Schlegel explains why this is so: "Injustice and greed would be the real thing if we lived forever. As it is, we must hold to other things, because Death is coming. I love Death—not morbidly, but because He explains. He shows me the emptiness of Money. Death and Money are the eternal foes. Not Death and Life."

Death and Money—death and a money-civilization from which the roots of life have been removed. Mr. Lucas lives, but in a way so base that we grieve he did not die. It could be objected, of course, that a petulant and degraded old age can come in any civilization and that the Greeks whom Forster so often invokes dreaded old age extravagantly. But this would not be to the point, which is that death and the value of the good life are related, that death is in league with love to support life: death, indeed, is what creates love. This is what Wordsworth is saying rather obscurely in his Immortality Ode: it is the thought of death that makes the meanest flower that blows bring thoughts that do often lie too deep for tears. The meanest thing is valuable to a mortal man, as the proudest thing could not be to an immortal.

The nature of death in Forster's novels has often been commented on; it is invariably sudden and invariably told about in the most casual way. But this is not, as one critic suggests, merely a bad habit. It is deeply related to Forster's view of life and it is significant that not only in "The Road to Colonus" but in two other of the early stories Forster has already begun to deal with it. In "The Point of It," a grim fantasy, one young man's early death in a spurt of physical energy is glorified as against his friend's living out a mildly honored life of respectable compromise. And in "The Story of the Siren," perhaps the best of the fantastic stories, the siren is death, and the young man who sees her in the Caves of the Sea becomes unhappy to the point of madness because he knows that every living thing must die; yet he marries a girl who has also seen the siren, and it is prophesied of their child that he will fetch up the siren into the air for all to see. "And thus, the prophecy goes on, the world will be saved." But the girl who was carrying this unborn savior was, at the instance of a priest, pushed into the sea and drowned.

Death punctuates all of Forster's novels and it is not until *A Passage to India* that he suggests that death is anything but benign, and even here his judgment is at least ambiguous. Mrs. Moore's vision of death in the Marabar Caves breaks and perhaps deteriorates her; nullity and the void are too much for her, but it is hinted that some good is to come of her despair. Roger Fry, in a letter quoted in Virginia Woolf's biography of him, wrote of *A Passage to India*, "I think it's a marvelous texture—really beautiful writing. But Oh

Lord I wish he weren't a mystic, or that he would keep his mysticism out of his books." Fry was wrong about his old friend—Forster is not a mystic in any precise sense of the word. Yet there is an element in his work that does give the appearance of mysticism: it is his sense of life being confronted by death. A money-civilization chooses not to consider this confrontation; it is one of our most pertinacious refusals and we support it by calling "mystical" anyone who does consider it.

The theme of the inadequacy of modern civilization, implied in "The Road from Colonus," is dealt with explicitly in the second of Forster's non-fantastic stories. "The Eternal Moment" is about a middle-aged novelist, Miss Raby, who after many years is visiting the Alpine town where, in her youth, she had had what seemed a trivial love adventure. A young man, a porter and guide, had put his pack down on the road and declared his love. The Miss Raby of years before had acted the insulted lady and the young fellow had apologized; the incident had ended. But like other such incidents in Forster's plots, it had not ended at all. And Miss Raby has another connection with the town, for tourists had "discovered" it when she had described and named it in her successful novel and the town had become prosperous. With prosperity had come corruption and crassness. The immemorial peasant life had been transformed to take advantage of the tourist trade. The old warm simplicity had chilled into the swank and the aggression of class—of money-class and of snobbery, the eternal vice which so particularly marks the "modern" era of any civilization, the vice which Forster was to find even in India.

. . . Sexually, [Aziz] was a snob. This had puzzled and worried Fielding. Sensuality, as long as it is straightforward, did not repel him, but this derived sensuality—the sort that classes a mistress among motor cars if she is beautiful, and among eye-flies if she isn't—was alien to his own emotions, and he felt a barrier between himself and Aziz whenever it arose. It was, in a new form, the old, old trouble that eats the heart out of every civilization: snobbery, the desire for possessions, creditable appendages; and it is to escape this rather than the lusts of the flesh that saints retreat into the Himalayas.

Miss Raby, a passionate democrat, feels that it is through her that the little town had so sadly altered. Her horror of the new town runs parallel with her recollection of the young porter's offer of love: her response to his declaration has sprung not only from an as yet undeveloped heart but also from her sense of class. She seeks out her former admirer. The athletic Italian porter has become the fat concierge of the most glittering of the new hotels. His gauche impulsiveness has given way to the diplomacy of the hotel lobby. When she recalls to him the vanished moment of their youth, he is at first frightened of blackmail, then he thinks her lewd. And she, desperate that a generous heart should have so dried and that a human town should have become an emptiness, makes of him the extraordinary request that he give her one of his children so that he may be reared free from the killing "stupidity" of the modern snob-world. He thinks her mad. And in this Miss Raby's traveling companion, up to that moment perhaps to be her husband, the intelligent and chaste Colonel Leyland, quite agrees with the vulgar hotel official. From the snob-world, the world of the undeveloped heart, of no-feeling or of only class-feeling, death is the only escape. And it is to old age and death that Miss Raby turns for comfort in her despair.

Here, then, in these early stories are the clearly stated themes which Forster will develop through his career as a novelist—the basic theme of the inadequate heart, the themes of the insufficient imagination, of death, money, snobbery and salvation. And not only are Forster's persisting themes announced in these early works but also the character types which we shall encounter in all his novels. Thus Miss Raby is the delicate ancestress of Forster's most notable heroines, women elderly, or middle-aged, or moving toward middle age—Mrs. Wilcox of *Howards End* and Margaret Schlegel of the same novel, Rickie's dead mother in *The Longest Journey,* Mrs. Moore of *A Passage to India.* She is the woman wise but powerless, in some way triumphant, in some way defeated, often confused yet gifted with an obscure certainty, as if remembering some ancient sibylline wisdom that the world no longer knows. Although three of the heroines are mothers of sons, their connections with their sons are tenuous. Mrs. Wilcox is far removed from her Paul and Charles, who are quite of another spirit; so is Mrs. Moore from her Ronny. Mrs. Wilcox finds her heir in Margaret Schlegel, Mrs. Moore finds a truer son than Ronny in Dr. Aziz.

The implication seems to be that the sons have betrayed their mothers. Yet actually the mothers have remarkably little impulse toward their sons. Mrs. Wilcox seems never to have had a vital connection with Charles and Paul, which perhaps accounts for the masculine stupidity of the two men; Mrs. Moore is so easily alienated from Ronny and her tie with him so quickly broken that she seems never to have had an animal relation with him at all; Rickie Elliot's mother, although very tender, was late in coming to love her son and never seems wholly attached to him. Margaret Schlegel, Mrs. Wilcox's "heir," declares that she does not love or want children. In the counter-Wellsian fantasy of the future life, "The Machine Stops," it is the son who sins against the mechanical dispensation by discovering the forbidden filial affection; his mother does not match it with maternal feeling. This remote quality in Forster's elder heroines must check our natural tendency to find in them a symbol of the Earth which man has deserted (although the Earth-Mother identification is explicit in "The Machine Stops"). Appealing and good as these heroines are, they lack maternal warmth: perhaps it is dissatisfaction with their husbands that has turned them from their sons, though that is not the usual course of things; or perhaps what is responsible for the failure of normal maternal affection is the early rupture of the family tie by the public school, a thwarting of the normal family life that Forster deplores in *The Longest Journey*—in some way these modern Demeters have not only transcended sex, like the ancient goddess of whom Forster wrote on his Greek tour, but they have also transcended some kinds of love and our response to them is partly pity.

"The Eternal Moment" first sketches the type of the wise and gentle heroine who is to descend from Miss Raby; "The Road from Colonus" gives us our first example of the woman who is to be contrasted with her. Ethel Lucas, when her father is lifted on to his saddle by a Mr. Graham of the party, sighs that she "admires strength"; she is the progenitor of Forster's sadistic women. Agnes Pembroke of *The Longest Journey,* with her secret pleasure at the idea of the big strong boy bullying the little weak one; or Mrs. Failing of the same novel who will torture any defenseless person; or Mrs. Herriton of *Where Angels Fear to Tread* who breaks out of gentility with curses; or Mrs. Herriton's daughter Harriet whom religion fortifies in fierceness—all these will follow the sadistic pattern. The type will be institutionalized in *A Passage to India* in the wives of the English officials who regard the Indians with a vindictive cruelty which is usually absent from their husbands' feeling and which is said to constitute one of the major emotional difficulties of administration.

One other feminine type must be mentioned, the heroine that Forster seems to have taken over from Meredith. Appearing first as Evelyn Beaumont of "Other Kingdom"—who turns into a tree to escape her stuffy, possessive lover—she will recur as Lucy Honeychurch of *A Room with a View* and, somewhat modified, as Helen Schlegel of *Howards End.* Wholly feminine, natural, simple, passionate, right, this is the heroine trapped and in need of rescue by a man.

And as for Forster's men, they too are outlined for us in these first two stories. In the main, Forster's male characters will descend either from the young porter of "The Eternal Moment" or from Colonel Leyland. The porter is the ancestor of all the athletic young heroes whose physical beauty and strength are their spiritual grace. The first of the line may be defeated and corrupt, but in his later avatars he is triumphant and brings salvation. Gino of *Where Angels Fear to Tread* is one of his descendants, although in Gino money-vulgarity is absorbed into his general vitality. George Emerson of *A Room with a View* is the same young man endowed with a brain and sensibility, and Stephen Wonham of *The Longest Journey* is yet another manifestation, equipped with an English conscience. The hearts, or the brains, or the consciences of these young men are nourished by their physical life; they have the gift of love and, as old Mr. Emerson says in *A Room with a View*, "Love is of the body—not the body, but of the body."

The Pans of Forster's fantastic stories state, in various ways, this eternal lesson. Modern life—it is to be D. H. Lawrence's theme— can kill the masculine power and tenderness; Pan inhabits the woods and fields which men have forsaken. That is why Gino must be a provincial Italian and Stephen a rustic, just as Stephen's dead father had been a farmer who saved with love a loving and unhappy woman. George Emerson is of the city and he is a prey to philosophical despair, but he is freed by nakedness and sunlight. Inhabiting the woods and fields, Pan can bring about the liberation of an adolescent boy ("The Story of a Panic") or the salvation of a formerly facetious and insincere clergyman ("The Curate's Friend").

Colonel Leyland is the faint prototype of the man who betrays the female spirit. He combines a certain enlightened official insensitivity with an old-maidish fussiness. The old-maidishness will turn up in Philip Herriton and, in *A Room with a View*, in Cecil Vyse. The insensitivity is to appear in Herbert Pembroke and Gerald Dawes of *The Longest Journey*, in the Wilcox men of *Howards End* and in Ronny of *A Passage to India*.

These men and women, some of them shaped for greatness, some of them born for quiet, mediocre lives, are constantly being led through trifles to a confrontation with the largest possible matters. I have mentioned the part which death plays in the novels; there is also the portentous theme which I. A. Richards speaks of as the "survival theme"—"a special preoccupation, almost an obsession, with the continuance of life." Appearing first, in "The Eternal Moment," in the strange request Miss Raby makes of the concierge, that he give her one of his children to bring up, it dominates *Where Angels Fear to Tread*, a novel in which the great struggle is for the ownership of a baby, and in which parenthood is the strongest passion; or it appears in *The Longest Journey*, in the use made of Stephen Wonham's little girl and in the repeated play with the themes of heredity; or again in *Howards End*, with the son of Leonard Bast and Helen Schlegel, who is to inherit the disputed house. Even in *A Passage to India* the children of Mrs. Moore's second marriage are introduced to carry on, in some way, their mother's spirit.

It would appear that the theme of survival supplements the theme of death, and serves to heighten in Forster's work the effect of what Roger Fry called "mysticism." But if mysticism is not the word, the right word is hard to find. We might say of Forster's ideas that they are marked by a natural and naturalistic piety. This is a difficult emotion to deal with; there is always the danger of a lapse into religiosity: an 18th-century deistic sentimentality lies in wait for the writer who expresses large emotions about life and death, even if he is determined to be wholly naturalistic. With orthodox religion as an expression of natural piety Forster has considerable sympathy and in *The Longest Journey* and *A Room with a View* he deals tenderly with it. Yet he always regards with hostility the repressive morality of orthodoxy and his bitterness against the clergy is unremitting. In the short stories, the clergy is represented as stupid or trifling ("The Story of a Panic," "The Curate's Friend") or as malign ("The Story of the Siren"); later, the Harriet Herriton of *Where Angels Fear to Tread,* the Mr. Eager and the Mr. Beebe of *A Room with a View,* the imperialistic parsons at Simpson's in *Howards End,* the pointless missionaries of *A Passage to India* will all continue to express Forster's antipathy to organized faith.

As far back as 1920, Katherine Mansfield, in a review of "The Story of the Siren,"[2] spoke in protest against the omnipresence of clergymen, in company with spinsters, in Forster's writing. "Mr. Forster's novels are alive with aunts and black with chaplains," she wrote, and went on to wonder "why there must always be, on every adventure, an aunt and a warbling chaplain. Why must they always be there in the boat, bright, merciless, clad from head to foot in the armour of efficiency?" We may reply that as often as truth, fertility and sensuality are to have their opposites, aunts and chaplains must, in the logic of Forster's imagination, appear on the scene.

---

[2] The story appeared in a pamphlet of the Hogarth Press. Katherine Mansfield's review appeared (over her initials) in *The Athenaeum* of August 13.

Yet all the characters of Forster's fiction are in the shadow of religion, the complex and "advanced" people as well as the simple.
Whatever their mature beliefs, they will all have been brought up
in an atmosphere suffused with religious feeling—after all, they were
born in the 19th century, in a time when, in *Robert Elsmere,* a young
man's religious difficulties and his liberalistic solution of them could
charm millions of readers. It is appropriate, too, that these people
who are still in the late 19th-century tradition of religion should find
their largest emotions not in religion itself but in art, for, in the
19th century, art was raised nearly to the level of religion and endowed with a quasi-religious function.

And this is an insight for which Forster is perhaps unique among
modern novelists—his understanding of the part played by art in
the life of the middle classes. On the one hand, art is salvation and
Forster appeals again and again to the freedom of imagination and
to the disinterestedness of the true lover of art. But on the other
hand, if art approaches religion, then its cultivation can approach
the religious vices of hypocrisy, respectability and mere piousness,
and Forster is the anatomist of the British tourist, with his Baedeker
and his Alinari prints, and of the British intellectual with his Pater,
his Symonds, and his Symons. He understands that art can be the
instrument of an enormous snobbery and he enjoys the comedy of
this fact; he knows, as we all know when we enter the perfectly
decorated room, that taste can be an aggressive weapon.

And so, defender of the arts as he is, Forster cultivates a deep
suspicion of good taste and is even inclined to find in tastelessness a
kind of benevolence and vitality. The first defense of tastelessness,
or even of bad taste, occurs in "The Eternal Moment" when Forster
remarks that a Carlo Dolce or a Carracci, "a debased style—so the
superior person and the textbooks say," is sometimes preferable to a
Fra Angelico. He loves the baroque, even the sentimental baroque,
and in *Where Angels Fear to Tread* he speaks affectionately of its
manifestations in Italian bad taste.

There is something majestic in the bad taste of Italy; it is not the bad
taste of a country which knows no better; it has not the nervous vulgarity

of England, or the blinded vulgarity of Germany. It observes beauty and chooses to pass it by. But it attains to beauty's confidence.

Or in *A Room with a View,* Mr. Flack's ugly villas and Lucy's ugly but pleasant house are defended against the good taste of Cecil Vyse; in *The Longest Journey* the family of Stewart Ansell is said to live happily together not because it has a community of taste but because it has no taste at all, while Mr. Elliot, who has perfect taste, is petty, mean and cruel. Life in its generous and vital aspects, Forster seems to be saying, is seldom tasteful.

The true lovers of art in Forster are those who truly love life, and they are beset by those who love art aggressively, or by those who love it officially. Such a person is the cultivated Mildred of "Albergo Empedocle" who, when she is brought to believe that her stupid lover had really lived in ancient Acragas, cries out, "O marvelous idea! . . . I should run about, shriek, sing. Marvelous! Overwhelming! How can you be so calm! The mystery! and the poetry, oh, the poetry!" But the stolid Harold, who has really had the experience, replies, "I don't see any poetry. It just happened, that's all." And all Mildred's "culture" requires that she claim an equal distinction: "Harold, I too have lived in Acragas," she says, but Harold, although he adores her, replies, "No, Mildred darling, you have not." That she should thus appear a shifty, shallow hypocrite infuriates her and she sets out to destroy Harold. Similarly, the artist of "The Story of a Panic" loves art in the wrong ways. He is aggressive and superior about his "advanced" aesthetic ideas and he makes them official and false; and it is he who betrays the adolescent hero. So too Mr. Bons, the cultured churchwarden of "The Celestial Omnibus" affirms his belief in "the essential truth of poetry," by which he means he does not believe in it at all; when he is led by a little boy to the Heaven of poetry, this merely cultured man is so frightened by the shield of Achilles that he falls to earth and is found dead near the Bermondsey gas works.

These, then, are the dominant themes, the stuff out of which Forster will build his novels. What no summary can suggest is the complication with which the novels will treat them. As they appear first in the short stories, they are not especially impressive. They have to be attached to complex characters and situations and they require the infinite modulation which Forster is later able to contrive.

Forster's short stories, indeed, are on the whole not successful, and their interest lies not so much in themselves as in their connection with the novels. For one thing, their tone is usually imperfect, though from this charge I would exempt "The Road from Colonus," "The Eternal Moment," and "The Story of the Siren." Three of the six stories of *The Celestial Omnibus* are narrated by what is in effect the same character, a very respectable person, small, timid, compromising, who nevertheless vaguely sees the true sanctities and obscurely wants to defend them; and the tone of this unfortunate person somehow pervades all the stories, giving them what Edward Shanks, writing of the style of Forster's *Pharos and Pharillon,* has cruelly but accurately called a quality of "demurely bloodless gaiety."

Something of this tone results from the nature of the fantasy Forster uses. In *Aspects of the Novel,* he skillfully defends fantasy, although as one of the legitimate ways of serious thought fantasy needs no apology. And one knows what Forster is doing with his heavens and hells, his dryads and Pans; we may say of him what Rickie in *The Longest Journey* says of Mr. Jackson, "He tries to express all modern life in the terms of Greek mythology, because the Greeks looked very straight at things and Demeter or Aphrodite are thinner veils than 'The survival of the fittest,' or 'A marriage has been arranged,' and other draperies of modern journalese." But Forster's mythology is inappropriate to his theme. It is the most literary and conventionalized of all mythologies and in modern hands the most likely to seem academic and arch, and it generates a tone which is at war with the robust intention of the stories. Fortunately Forster was to find a device better than, though akin to, fantasy and allegory; in his first novel he was to discover plot and thus give to his ideas a power which fantasy, much as he loved it, could never give.

CHAPTER FOUR

Where Angels Fear to Tread

FORSTER'S first novel appeared in 1905. The author was twenty-six, not a remarkable age at which to have written a first novel unless the novel be, as Forster's was, a whole and mature work dominated by a fresh and commanding intelligence.

It was a good time for intelligence. It was a good time for writing in general, but especially for writing in which the intelligence dominated. If we look at some of the great books published between 1902 and 1906—Butler's *The Way of All Flesh,* Bradley's *Shakespearean Tragedy,* William James's *The Varieties of Religious Experience,* Henry James's *The Wings of the Dove, The Ambassadors* and *The Golden Bowl,* Shaw's *Man and Superman,* Hardy's *The Dynasts*— we find that great intelligence is common to them all, a faculty of generalship, an ability to marshal multitudes of ideas for combat. The literary intelligence was prouder in those days and glittered more, and it is perhaps significant that in 1905 Conan Doyle was forced to bring Sherlock Holmes back to life, for Holmes embodied the great popular myth of the mind, he was the man to whom all things spoke. And the earth and humanity seemed then to be speaking to writers with an admonitory but articulate voice.

This quality of intelligence in Forster's first novel and in all his novels makes them difficult to deal with critically. To summarize any good, developed idea is to betray it; we must have not only its conclusions but its dialectical growth, and we must have its modifications. Forster's novels proceed in two ways—by means of complex and detailed plots which produce a long series of small or great shocks, and by means of the author's pronouncements, for the novels are "wise," they never hesitate to formulate and comment. This requires that they be considered in some detail.

But *Where Angels Fear to Tread* is a work of its time in other ways than in its use of the dialectical intelligence. It is a novel of learning and growth, like *The Way of All Flesh* and *The Ambassadors,* and, like them, a novel of broken ties. It is a story of questioning, disillusionment and conversion. It is a criticism of the great middle class. It is a novel of sexuality.

Its theme, like that of *The Ambassadors,* is the effect of a foreign country and a strange culture upon insular ideas and provincial personalities. Since the Renaissance, and especially in the 18th century, it had been a device of moralists to confront their own culture with the superior habits of foreign lands. And in the 19th century, the great age of travel, the century of Cook and his tourists, it became possible to see for oneself whether they really did order these things better in France—or in Italy or Germany or Spain. The investigation had two results. The middle classes learned that only in England, or America, were things ordered at all—the boast that Mussolini was to make, that his trains ran on time, was a barefaced appeal to the middle-class tourist. But the intellectuals surrendered gratefully to the ways of the strange country and were confirmed in their criticism of their own culture. The charm they found was no doubt sentimental, but it was also moral. An unknown people is not only quaint but also good. Forster tells us why: ". . . The barrier of language is sometimes a blessed barrier, which only lets pass what is good. Or—to put it less cynically—we may be better in clean words, which have never been tainted by pettiness or vice." In recent years a notable instance of the moral effect of a strange language is Ernest Hemingway's Spanish novel, *For Whom the Bell Tolls.*

The story of *Where Angels Fear to Tread* begins in a comedy of

manners, goes on to fierceness and melodrama and ends in an enlightened despair. For some years the Herriton family has had the
care of Lilia, the widow of the family's eldest son. Lilia is a grown
woman of thirty-three, but she is vulgar and the Herritons are
genteel. Her ten-year-old daughter has been largely removed from
her control and her attempts to enliven Sawston have put her quite
in the wrong. Now, after a long bondage and as the story opens,
Lilia has won a year of freedom in Italy, chaperoned by Miss Caroline Abbott, a girl ten years her junior but known in Sawston society
for her respectability and level head.

Poor Lilia is truly vulgar and silly—her "one qualification for life
was rather blowsy high spirits, which turned boisterous or querulous
according to circumstances." A lesser novelistic intelligence than
Forster's would have made her dashing or sensitive so that the
Herritons would seem more culpable, but they are quite culpable
enough in their domineering superiority, as unpleasant a family as
one can imagine. Mrs. Herriton, beneath her ·genteel manner, is a
person of great violence and her face can become distorted with
mean and terrible rage. With "her diplomacy, her insincerity, her
continued repression of vigour," she had made her life meaningless
and had become a "well-ordered, active, useless machine," able to
inspire her children with fear but not with reverence. She has let
her children go their ways, yet she has subtly dominated them, ruining her daughter and all but ruining her son. Harriet is a Low
Church fanatic, a dull Cassandra; her brother Philip once said of
her that she had "bolted all the cardinal virtues and couldn't digest
them."

As for Philip, he has managed to protect himself by priggishness
and aestheticism. He is as nearly impossible as it is possible for the
hero of a novel to be.

He was a tall, weakly built young man, whose clothes had to be ju-
diciously padded on the shoulders in order to make him pass muster. His
face was plain rather than not, and there was a curious mixture in it of
good and bad. He had a fine forehead and a good large nose, and both

observation and sympathy were in his eyes. But below the nose and eyes all was confusion, and those people who believe that destiny resides in the mouth and chin shook their heads when they looked at him.

He had a sense of beauty and a sense of humor, but the humor had turned aloof and sour; and the sense of beauty, into which "all the energies and enthusiasm of a rather friendless life had passed," was used chiefly to condemn the life and the people about him. Italy had first developed Philip's sense of beauty, and his sense of humor is gratified by the idea of the vulgar Lilia in that beloved land.

But the vulgar Lilia is to be more than amusing. So far from not being responsive to Italy, she has taken the country all too seriously and it appears that she is actually planning to marry there. Her fiancé, she says, is of noble birth, but the Herritons, naturally suspicious, are right in supposing that she lies. Mrs. Herriton dispatches Philip—he is in a painful position because "for three years he had sung the praises of Italians, but he had never contemplated having one as a relative"—to break off the match. He arrives at the little town of Monteriano to discover that things are worse than he had supposed. Lilia has engaged herself to a boy twelve years younger than she, not only not noble but not even genteel. He is the son of a dentist—and at this news

Philip gave a cry of personal disgust and pain. He shuddered all over. . . . A dentist! A dentist at Monteriano! A dentist in fairyland! False teeth and laughing gas and the tilting chair at a place which knew the Etruscan League and the Pax Romana and Alaric himself, and the Countess Matilda, and the Middle Ages, all fighting and holiness, and the Renaissance, all fighting and beauty. He thought of Lilia no longer. He was anxious for himself: he feared that Romance might die.

This moment of absurd disillusionment is the first step in Philip's education. The novelist comments:

Romance only dies with life. No pair of pincers will ever pull it out of us. But there is a spurious sentiment which cannot resist the unexpected and incongruous and the grotesque. A touch will loosen it, and the sooner it goes from us the better. It was going from Philip now, and therefore he gave a cry of pain.

But the immediate effect of the pain is to make Philip even stupider and more unpleasant than before. He loathes Lilia's young Gino Carella, so clearly not a gentleman, and he is arrogant and rude to him. And Gino, indeed, is no gentleman, nor even quite a moral person. When Philip offers him a thousand lire to give up Lilia, it is not at all an easy decision for him to make; over his beautiful face pass many conflicting emotions, "avarice, insolence, politeness, stupidity and cunning." But actually he is no longer free to make a choice—he and Lilia are already married.

There is nothing now to do save leave the married couple to themselves. And Lilia, left to herself in the little provincial Italian town, is far more miserable than she had ever been in Sawston. D. H. Lawrence, in *The Lost Girl,* was to use the situation of an Englishwoman married in Italy to an Italian below her station; he was to evoke a complex and triumphant sexuality, but Forster's Lilia is not sexual and whatever feelings she at first had for her young husband soon pass with boredom. There is almost no society in Monteriano, and what little there is Gino is not willing for her to see: in Italy there exists for men "that true Socialism which is based not on equality of income or character, but on the equality of manners," but it exists at the expense of the sisterhood of women. Gino asserts an Italian husband's authority and on the one occasion when his wife challenges it, his rage is so literally blind and so terrible that she never tries again. Nor has she any way of dealing with his early infidelity. Once she tries to escape, only to be brought home kindly and inexorably by her young husband.

She did not hate him, even as she had never loved him; with her it was only when she was excited that the semblance of either passion arose. People said she was headstrong, but really her weak brain left her cold. Suffering, however, is more independent of temperament, and the wisest of women could hardly have suffered more.

As for Gino, he neither loves nor hates. He is normally lustful but never really passionate in his sexuality. He had only one desire—

to become the father of a man like himself, and it held him with a grip he only partially understood, for it was the first great desire, the first grand passion of his life. Falling in love was a mere physical triviality, like warm sun or cool water, beside the divine hope of immortality: "I continue."

This desire of Gino's—this manifestation of the "survival theme" —is to dominate the novel. At last the hapless Lilia gives birth to a child.

[Gino] lay outside the room with his head against the door like a dog. When they came to tell him the glad news they found him half unconscious, and his face wet with tears.

As for Lilia, some one said to her, "It is a beautiful boy!" But she had died in giving birth to him.

Lilia's death in childbirth is the first of the sudden, unmotivated deaths in Forster's novels.

In the preceding chapter I have tried to suggest the place that death holds in the logic of Forster's imagination. But something must be said of the brusque casualness, the lack of "reason" and "motivation" which invariably marks his deaths.

One thing to say is that certain kinds of unmotivated events in fiction represent what happens in life. Life is not only a matter of logic and motivation but of chance. The storyteller may—perhaps should—suggest this element of life, the only restriction being that he abstain from "solving" a given "problem" by the agency of chance. What Thomas Hardy called "crass casualty"[1] has its place in human existence. In Forster's world death gives a peculiar emphasis to life and it is the essence of the drama of death that it so often is crassly casual.

Another justification of Forster's use of sudden death is aesthetic: it is a useful device for his contrivance of plot. Just as in a game of chess, the value of all the pieces on the board may be changed by the removal of a single piece, the forces shifting and the game entering a new phase, so in a novel of a certain integration the death of any integral character may alter the value and the situation

---

[1] The phrase is quoted by Jacques Barzun in "Truth and Poetry in Thomas Hardy" (*The Southern Review*, Summer, 1940). The essay is a defense of Hardy's "lack of motivation." "The truth is," says Mr. Barzun, "we blame Hardy for failing to show adequate cause when the lack of adequate cause is what Hardy is trying to show."

of all the other characters. Our modern taste does not approve a metaphor which compares the novel to a game. In serious literature we do not want, we consider childish, the play of wit and ingenuity that makes a work of art our friendly opponent, pleasing us by outwitting us. We have, that is, turned away from plot, and in doing so we have lost an immemorial aid to thought.

Forster in his *Aspects of the Novel* says that "the plot . . . is the novel in its logical intellectual aspect." It represents the novelist's interest in causality; it is, as he says, concerned with mystery. In his own practice, it involves all the old devices of recognition scenes, secrets, letters that prove something, stolen babies, destroyed wills, long-lost brothers, hidden sins, shocking revelations and even physical conflict. A critic has written of Forster as a "contemplative novelist"; perhaps he is, but he contemplates by means of hot melodrama.

And here again the average contemporary taste draws back, insisting that life is not like that, that life does not work by secrets and revelations. But even granting that life is not like that, a concession to mediocrity I am not at all sure should be made, it is still possible to justify novels that use plot as Forster's do.

For plot is to the novelist what experiment is to the scientist, which is exactly what Zola did not know when he wrote his essay "The Experimental Novel"; Zola's defense of scientific naturalism in fiction has nothing at all to do with experiment. The science he had in mind as analogous to novel-writing was medicine as practised by the great physician Claude Bernard; that is to say, he had in mind an empirical, not an experimental, science. And Zola's novelistic "science" was a science of observation, and precisely not of experiment. He condemned plot as artificial, but experiment is artificial too—nature does not exist in test-tubes and retorts and under controlled conditions, and to conclude that what happens in the laboratory is what happens in the universe requires a leap of the imagination. But experiment, with its artificiality, is our best way of making things act so that we can learn about their nature. And plot in the novel does the same for human nature.

The authority of Aristotle need count for nothing as we recall that he said that the one thing necessary for drama was plot; but he was right. Miss Dorothy Richardson tells us that this does not apply to the novel and calls Joyce and Proust to witness. But Joyce based his most successful novel on one of the most successful of melodramas, the *Odyssey,* and Proust, if seen entire, as he should be, is melodramatic from beginning to end, while Miss Richardson's own contempt of plot makes for the willful exhibitionism of her own novel: it is a virtue of plot that it keeps the personality of the novelist within bounds.

Ideas and moral essences are, to all people, the most interesting things in the world, and the popular taste is quite right in knowing that what best expresses these things is not characters and not emotions, but actions: all plots are ideas, but not all people are ideas. Then too, plot can give people dignity, making them heroes and heroines, or lay them bare of pretense, making them villains or poltroons. Or plot, because it is concerned not only with states of being but with consequences, gives the greatest reality to social forces. It suggests, more vividly than any naturalistic novel can, the social connection of individuals.

But I have left Forster's novel on the brink of its plot. To the Herritons in England the news of Lilia's baby is a nuisance and a danger. Soon Irma Herriton, Lilia's English daughter, begins to receive postcards, one of them improper, from her "lital brother" in Italy. This is a blow; the Herritons had hoped to keep the news of the child secret not only from Irma but from all Sawston. Gino is written to and ordered to cease communication but the secret is out and its deepest effect is upon Caroline Abbott, Lilia's former chaperone. She had, she tells Philip, been responsible for Lilia's marriage. Drunk with rebellion in Italy, she had hated Sawston for its idleness, stupidity, respectability and petty unselfishness. ("Petty selfishness," Philip corrects her. "Petty unselfishness," she insists and immediately becomes the heroine of the novel.) She herself could not escape but she had urged Lilia to take the offered chance. And now she is filled with remorse; she feels that she is the cause of

Lilia's unhappiness and death. There is one way of atonement. The child must be brought to England and properly reared.

And in this the Herritons concur; they say it is what they themselves want although actually they have no desire for the child. But Caroline now has a moral purpose beyond anything she had ever felt in her church charity work. Her passion both affronts and shames the Herritons. They make an offer to Gino through their solicitors and are relieved when it is refused. Caroline, however, sees through their insincerity and offers to go to Italy at her own expense. At this Mrs. Herriton takes vulgar offense and dispatches Philip—who has been behaving like an old gossip—to fetch the Carella baby. And because the baby must now really be had, Caroline having made such an issue of it, and because Mrs. Herriton knows that Philip's heart is not in the venture, she orders Philip to pick up his sister Harriet who is summering in one of the Protestant cantons of Switzerland.

The brother and sister make a dreadful trip, Harriet filled with rage and scorn and moral fervor, Philip trying to enjoy his Italy. To their surprise, Caroline Abbott has come to Monteriano before them. "Spy or traitor?" Philip challenges her, and the increasingly remarkable young woman answers, "Spy." For Mrs. Herriton had behaved insincerely and dishonorably, not wanting the child, yet acting as if she did; Caroline is here to help the Herritons if they really try for the baby, or to get it herself if they do not.

But Caroline's own purpose has somehow changed. She has had an interview with Gino and he has not been quite the beast she knows him to be. And Philip's own moral fibre is further weakened when she mentions that Gino has expressed his regret for his rudeness of the last visit; Philip's old love of Italy returns—"there were no cads in her; she was beautiful, courteous, lovable, as of old."

Harriet, however, is not in the least weakened. Unapproachable by any amenity, she is firm in her religious duty and demands that things be settled immediately. Gino must be taught English business methods. But Gino has gone away for the day and that evening there takes place an incident which advances Philip's education a step further. The English party go to the performance of *Lucia di Lammermoor* at the little local theatre. The scene is a great one and carries the novel to the heights of comic bravura. It begins with a description of the theatre which has been lately done up in tints of tomato and beet-root, calling forth the comment, already quoted, on the vital bad taste of Italy. "This tiny theatre of Monteriano spraddled and swaggered with the best of them, and these ladies [painted on the proscenium arch] with their clock would have nodded to the young men of the Sistine." Miss Abbott is charmed and she is sorry that she has not brought any pretty clothes: something has indeed happened to her moral fibre. But Harriet remains firm and dominates the house. For the audience accompanies the opening chorus with "tappings and drummings, swaying in the melody like corn in the wind. Harriet, though she did not care for music, knew how to listen to it. She uttered an acid 'Shish!'" The house becomes quiet, "not because it is wrong to talk during a chorus but because it is natural to be civil to a visitor." Harriet has turned "this great evening party into a prayer meeting"; Sawston has met Italy and has triumphed. But the audience is soon out of hand again and when the mad Lucia ("clad in white, as befitted her malady") ends her aria, it explodes into pleasure, shouts, kisses, flowers and a bouquet with a *billet doux* in it which hits poor Harriet. "Call this classical," she cries as she gets up. "It's not even respectable!" And it is in the midst of this wonderful *brio* that Philip meets Gino and is embraced by him as not only a friend but a relative, a brother-in-law, a brother.

It is a great event for Philip. He feels free and happy in the warm Italian holiday spirit of Gino and his friends. And feeling so, know-that Gino feels so, he is quite certain that Gino can have no attachment to the child, for he is English enough to suppose that love must be solemn. But Miss Abbott is soon to know otherwise. She calls on Gino and is admitted in his absence; she waits in the stiff, dull parlor that has been grimly consecrated to the dead Lilia. And as Gino enters, unaware of her presence, he leaves open the door of his room and she could see into it, right across the landing. It was in a shocking mess. Food, bedclothes, patent leather boots, dirty plates, and knives lay strewn over a large table and on the floor. But it was the mess that comes of life, not of desolation. It was preferable to the charnel-chamber in which she was standing now, and the light in it was soft and large, as from some gracious, noble opening.

In this living and nourishing mess is the child, and as the interview between Caroline and Gino develops, she learns what we have always known, that the child is the passion of Gino's life. Now for the first time she understands that the baby is real, a human being, not a principle.

She had thought so much about this baby, of its welfare, its soul, its morals, it probable defects. But, like most unmarried people, she had only thought of it as a word—just as the healthy man only thinks of the word death, not of death itself. The real thing, lying asleep on a dirty rug, disconcerted her. It did not stand for a principle any longer. It was so much flesh and blood, so many inches and ounces of life—a glorious, unquestionable fact, which a man and another woman had given to the world. You could talk to it; in time it would answer you; in time it would not answer you unless it chose, but would secrete, within the compass of its body, thoughts and wonderful passions of its own. And this was the machine on which she and Mrs. Herriton and Philip and Harriet had for the last month been exercising their various ideals—had determined that in time it should move this way or that way, should accomplish this and not that. It was to be Low Church, it was to be high-principled, it was to be tactful, gentlemanly, artistic—excellent things all. Yet now that she saw this baby, lying asleep on a dirty rug, she had a great disposition not to dictate one of them, and to exert no more influence than there may be in a kiss or in the vaguest of heartfelt prayers.

As she and Gino talk, "the horrible truth, that wicked people are capable of love, stood naked before her, and her moral being was abashed."

[Gino] stood with one foot resting on the little body, suddenly musing, filled with the desire that his son should be like him, and should have sons like him to people the earth. It is the strongest desire that can come to a man—if it comes to him at all—stronger even than love or the desire for personal immortality. All men vaunt it, and declare that it is theirs; but the hearts of most are set elsewhere. It is the exception who comprehends that physical and spiritual life may stream out of him for ever. Miss Abbott, for all her goodness, could not comprehend it, though such a thing is more within the comprehension of women.

And the survival theme continues:

It was too late to go. She could not tell why, but it was too late. She turned away her head when Gino lifted his son to his lips. This was something too remote from the prettiness of the nursery. The man was majestic; he was part of Nature; in no ordinary love scene could he ever be so great. For a wonderful physical tie binds the parents to the children; and—by some sad, strange irony—it does not bind us children to our parents. For if it did, if we could answer their love not with gratitude but with equal love, life would lose much of its pathos and much of its squalor, and we might be wonderfully happy. Gino passionately embracing, Miss Abbott reverently averting her eyes—both of them had parents whom they did not love so very much.

When Philip comes to make his offer for the baby, he finds Miss Abbott holding the child on her lap, drying it after its bath, while Gino watches—"to all intents and purposes, the Virgin and Child, with Donor."

Gino is to be the Donor in more senses than one, but Miss Abbott is to remain a virgin. So is Philip, for this strange little comic novel is to end in enlightened and bearable despair.

Yet before despair, there is tragedy and cruelty. Two of the English party now know they can never have the baby, and they are glad, for both of them have been influenced by Gino's elemental love for the child. But Harriet, the grim spirit of religion, untouched and untouchable by love, does not know, and she gets the baby. She steals it, just in time to catch the train out of Monteriano. Philip, unconscious of his sister's mad crime, believes that Gino, not so great a man as he had appeared, has, after all, sold the baby. On the way to the station the baby sickens; and, when the carriage overturns, it is dropped by Harriet and found dead. Philip, his arm broken in the accident, carries the news to Gino.

And now occurs the scene of horror which matches and balances the scene of joy at the opera. It is the crucial scene in the book—

crucial dramatically and crucial philosophically. Gino receives the news in terrible silence, then hurls the lamp out of the window and in the darkened room obscenely stalks Philip. When he catches him, he methodically tortures his broken arm and then carefully and slowly begins to choke him to death. The entrance of Caroline Abbott, gifted with great powers by a kind of transfiguration, saves Philip and even brings about the reconciliation of the two men.

The English critic, Mr. Montgomery Belgion, in his essay on Forster, asks, in a very strict manner, "What are Mr. Forster's values?" He answers that they are the values of the devil and his essay is called "The Diabolism of E. M. Forster." It turns out that Forster's diabolism consists of a dislike of modern parsons and certain doctrinal errors. But Mr. Belgion says nothing of Gino's torture of Philip. Yet in this act Gino is, as Philip cries in his pain, a devil. What are we to make of it? Are we being asked to believe that the power of love in Gino depends upon the coexistence of cruelty? Probably not. What Forster seems to be saying is that love arises from a generally passionate nature and depends upon a valuation of things so passionate as to quite overwhelm the reason, even to the point of cruelty. To judge Gino's cruelty, we must take the incident in its novelistic context; we must first set it beside Philip's profound indifference to life, then—for everything may be differentiated, even cruelty—we must compare it with the moral cruelty of Harriet, the genteel cruelty of Mrs. Herriton in England; and we must observe that, when the passion is over, Gino is ready not only to forgive but to love Philip. He is not a creature of tragedy, only of passion, and as the novel ends we learn that, once his sorrow is past, he will be happy again. This is perhaps shallowness, but many years later, in his war pamphlet, *Nordic Twilight,* Forster will find part of the German malady to lie in Germany's too great sense of the tragic in life. And he is right. For Gino may become temporarily a devil because he is a man; but Harriet is permanently a devil because she is not really a woman, as Mr. Elliot in *The Longest Journey* is permanently a devil because he is not at all a man. Gino's deviltry is the result of passion, not of principle and will, and it passes.

As for Philip, he is not quite a man, though he wishes to be. To
Philip, as to the hero of Henry James's "The Beast in the Jungle,"
nothing can ever happen; that is his tragedy. Before the climax of
the novel there is a devastating and rather dreadful scene between
him and Miss Abbott.

"You are wonderful!" he said bravely.

"Oh, you appreciate me!" she burst out again. "I wish you didn't. You
appreciate all of us. And all the time you are dead—dead—dead. Look,
why aren't you angry?" She came up to him, and then her mood suddenly changed, and she took hold of both his hands. "You are so splendid, Mr. Herriton, that I can't bear to see you wasted. I can't bear—she
has not been good to you—your mother."

"Miss Abbott, don't worry over me. Some people are born not to do
things. I'm one of them. . . . I don't die—I don't fall in love. And if
other people die or fall in love they always do it when I'm just not there.
You are quite right; life to me is just a spectacle, which—thank God,
and thank Italy, and thank you—is now more beautiful and heartening
than it has ever been before."

She said solemnly, "I wish something would happen to you, my dear
friend; I wish something would happen to you."

"But why?" he asked, smiling. "Prove to me why I don't do as I am."

She also smiled, very gravely. She could not prove it. No argument
existed. Their discourse, splendid as it had been, resulted in nothing. . . .

Eventually, in addition to God, Italy and Caroline Abbott, Philip
has Gino to thank for the spectacle of life being beautiful and heartening. But it still remains a spectacle; his salvation cannot be complete. On the trip back to England he proposes to Caroline, for
Gino has very explicitly directed Philip's eyes to her physical attrac-
tions. But she gently refuses him; she likes him but he is still an
uncommitted man. He is invalidated by Gino and she loves Gino,
physically, sexually, "because he's handsome." "I mean it crudely,"
she says, "—you know what I mean . . . Get over supposing I'm
refined. That's what puzzles you. Get over that." She has been
"saved" because, while she "was worshipping every inch of him,
and every word he spoke," Gino has thought of her as "a superior
being—a goddess." So, "saved," and with the knowledge that "all

the wonderful things are over," she condemns herself to a life that is at best endurable.

The novel ends with an almost intentional weakness, petering out in sad discourse. Yet its effect is invigorating. A point has been made, an idea developed. The life of self-complacency has been confronted with the life of self, and Sawston and its illusions can never again have their hold upon Caroline and Philip. We are not misled with false conversions on their part; the life of self with its healthy overflow of emotion is not for them and at best they can but understand it. Nor have we been misled by any overestimation of the life of self; Forster is not taken in by his Gino as Santayana is by his analogous Mario, and if he defends Mediterranean instinct against British cant or phlegm, he knows the limits of its value. The invigoration of the book comes from two ideas meeting and one of them being modified. Nothing important has been changed, but in the struggle things have assumed their right names and true meanings.

CHAPTER FIVE

The Longest Journey

O F FORSTER'S five novels, *The Longest Journey* is by conventional notions the least perfect—the least compact, the least precisely formed. Yet although Forster himself says that "it is a novel which most readers have dismissed as a failure," it is perhaps the most brilliant, the most dramatic and the most passionate of his works. In its arbitrary departures from the proprieties of the modern novel there is a genuine refreshment and even a special claim upon our affections. Those of us who respond to this claim will grant that the book is not a perfect whole, but we feel that it does not so much fall apart as fly apart: the responsive reader can be conscious not of an inadequate plan or of a defect in structure but rather of the too-much steam that blows up the boiler.

The story opens with a metaphysical discussion. A group of Cambridge undergraduates is belaboring the problem which fascinates all young students of philosophy, whether a thing really exists, really is *there,* if no observer is present to see it. One of the disputants, Stewart Ansell—he is not the hero but he is one of the heroic people in the story—insists that the cow (they have chosen a cow as example, rather than the table consecrated to such discussions) is really there; others disagree. They are not especially expert in their argument and they proceed chiefly by the reiteration of their opinions. The scene, delightful but apparently trivial, is a statement of what the story is about: it is about reality—appearance and reality—and the word "real" recurs again and again in the novel.

Few stories are metaphysical and few begin with metaphysical discussions, but many of the best stories deal with just this problem of appearance and reality. It is, indeed, one of the great themes of literature. It is what much of the *Odyssey* is about; *Oedipus Rex* and *Don Quixote* deal with it pre-eminently; it is Shakespeare's great subject in *Hamlet, Othello* and *Lear,* as well as in *Troilus and Cressida, The Winter's Tale* and *The Tempest;* it is the essential matter of *Faust;* it is everlastingly teasing Tolstoy. It is not "truth" that these stories deal with; reality is a more exact concept than truth and simple people are more interested in it than in truth; reality is the word we use for what can be relied on, felt, pushed against. It is what is thick, and lasts.

The discussion of reality is interrupted by the arrival of a young woman. She is the guest of the undergraduate who is host to the others. Rickie Elliot, having invited Agnes Pembroke and her brother Herbert for a visit, has quite forgotten to meet them or provide for them. Thus has his unconscious mind spoken for him, but he is unfortunately not to listen to his unconscious mind. Agnes enters, poised and voluble, dominating the group of embarrassed young men. Her first bright social words are of a horsewhipping for the forgetful Rickie. As unobtrusively as possible, all the undergraduates slip away, leaving only Stewart Ansell with Rickie and Agnes. Rickie introduces Ansell, Agnes puts out her hand in greeting, Ansell acts exactly as if she were not there and Agnes stands with outstretched unshaken hand. When Rickie later visits Ansell to scold him for this shocking rudeness, Ansell insists that he could not have been rude because no one was there. This, as Rickie points out, is both nonsense and at variance with Ansell's philosophic views about the cow, and Ansell replies:

Did it never strike you that phenomena may be of two kinds: *one,* those which have a real existence, such as the cow; *two,* those which are the subjective product of a diseased imagination, and which, to our destruction, we invest with the semblance of reality? If this never struck you, let it strike you now.

"Which, to our destruction, we invest with the semblance of reality" —so terrible can be the wrong notion of the real, and it is exactly to his own destruction that Rickie is to mistake its nature. In *Howards End* there is a reiterated phrase about the inner life, the life of true morality: it *pays,* says Forster, asserting in the coarsest available language what moralists always insist to be true, though they seldom convince us, partly because of the language they use. The inner life is real. *The Longest Journey* is about Rickie's loss of the inner life. By a terrible irony, he loses the inner life through his devotion to it.

As a type of hero, Rickie is by now familiar, even conventional. He has a touch of Joyce's Stephen Dedalus, but without the bitter force, a touch of Maugham's Philip Carey (for he has a club foot and an unhappy taste in women) but without Philip Carey's essential deadness, a touch of Samuel Butler's Ernest Pontifex, a touch of Lawrence's Paul Morel. Shy and craving love, he hates the memory of his father and adores the memory of his mother, has a certain literary talent, a great love of the beautiful, and a great fear of the practical life. He is, in short, the average sensitive young man of novels.

But Rickie is different from others of his type in one important respect. He has a dignity which comes from his being truly involved in the life of moral choice. The young man of the novels is usually devoted to learning something—he learns to be resistant, or contented, or to master his art. In some way he is made to triumph over circumstances by the process of mere growth. He *experiences* life— that is to say, he goes through events as if they were a tunnel, and our interest is in watching him come out safely at the other end. Usually the tunnel is a Tunnel of Horrors, but out he comes, inevitably and in the inevitable mood of chastened exaltation. But Rickie Elliot traces his descent not to the exasperating father of all the *Bildungsroman* heroes, Wilhelm Meister, but to the one young man who was truly great. Rickie is related to Julien Sorel. The life that Forster provides for Rickie is not a school; it is the real thing, like the life Stendhal provides for Julien. We know that life for these two young men is real and serious if only because it kills them both. For both authors have said: Experience be damned—life either pays or you die. And pays in hard, tangible coin.

Rickie's life is not a tunnel and he cannot "pass through" events. He becomes involved, and his choices have real consequences. He does not achieve knowledge—indeed, he begins with knowledge and loses it as he goes into life—but a kind of dignity.

The plot of *The Longest Journey* is extremely crowded with incident. A large part of the action takes place before the novel begins. We learn of the past events through devices that are sometimes ingenious enough and sometimes intentionally gauche.[1] As the events of the present move forward, they disclose the events of the past until past and present meet to produce the catastrophe. The past supplies many characters of the story, and one of the dead characters —there are no less than four—comments on life by means of a book of his which is in the course of being edited.

Rickie is the son of a loving mother and a hateful father. The mother is gentle and passionate, the father facetious, fastidious and cruel; like his only son, he has a deformity of the foot. Within a brief span both parents die suddenly in the Forster fashion, leaving Rickie fairly well off but eager for love, remembering his mother's affection and his father's hatefulness.

He marries Agnes Pembroke. She is older than he and stronger than he—stronger not only by reason of nature but also because her heart is not involved in the marriage, for her days of passion are behind her and Rickie is but a second best. Agnes had been engaged to Gerald Dawes, a young man in every way Rickie's opposite. Gerald had been stupid and conventional, athletic and peevish. One day Rickie chanced to overhear Gerald and Agnes in conversation;

---

[1] Rickie says to a group of friends: "I can't see why I shouldn't tell you most things about my birth and parentage and education." The friends reply: "Talk away. If you bore us, we have books." And the novelist: "With this invitation Rickie began to relate his history. The reader who has no book will be obliged to listen to it."

from the way they pecked and bickered he understood that they did not love each other. But this was only his undergraduate simplicity, for the cold dull tiff ended in a fierce kiss which, in Rickie's eyes, quite transfigured the pair. It seemed impossible to him that these two burning people should endure the pain and humiliation of a long engagement: he offered Gerald money to marry on, and Gerald—he had been brutal to Rickie at school—turned on him in violent rage.

Rickie's action was Shelleyan. The title of the novel is taken from *Epipsychidion*[2] and the theme of the book might well have been suggested by *Alastor*. The latter poem, as Shelley tells us in his preface, is about "a youth of uncorrupted feelings and adventurous genius" whose imagination is "inflamed and purified through all that was excellent and majestic." But he thirsts for intercourse with an intelligence similar to himself. "He seeks in vain for a prototype of his conception. Blasted by his disappointment, he descends to an untimely grave." This, Shelley tells us, is the retribution for his self-centered seclusion; the youth did what Ansell had warned Rickie against doing: to his destruction he had invested—or had tried to invest—with the semblance of reality the subjective product of a diseased imagination.

Yet—Shelley goes on—there is a worse fate, the "slow and poisonous decay [of] those meaner spirits" who, "deluded by no generous error, instigated by no sacred thirst of doubtful knowledge, duped

---

[2] Lines 149–159:

> I never was attached to that great sect,
> Whose doctrine is, that each one should select
> Out of the crowd a mistress or a friend,
> And all the rest, though fair and wise, commend
> To cold oblivion, though it is in the code
> Of modern morals, and the beaten road
> Which those poor slaves with weary footsteps tread,
> Who travel to their home among the dead
> By the broad highway of the world, and so
> With one chained friend, perhaps a jealous foe,
> The dreariest and longest journey go.

The thirty lines that follow are also pertinent to the novel. And in Rickie's emotional condition which results from his marriage to Agnes there are many similarities to Shelley's state of mind toward the end of his marriage to Mary, which is symbolically dealt with in *Epipsychidion*.

by no illustrious superstition, loving nothing on this earth, and cherishing no hopes beyond, yet keep aloof from sympathies with their kind, rejoicing neither in human joy nor mourning with human grief." They are "morally dead," they are "neither friends, nor lovers, nor fathers, nor citizens of the world"—they are "those unforeseeing multitudes who constitute, together with their own, the lasting misery and loneliness of the world."

This has a kind of noble despair about it—one is either blasted by devotion to an illustrious superstition which one endows with the semblance of reality or one is enrolled among the unforeseeing multitudes who slowly and poisonously decay. But *The Longest Journey* is written to show that such a tragic dilemma is not necessary. Rickie is the votary of generous error and illustrious superstition; he believes in high morality, in the inner life, in the goodness of man and, having at Cambridge turned his desires toward objects excellent and majestic, and having there had intercourse with male intelligences similar to himself, he seeks for the female prototype of his conception. He endows Agnes with the semblance of reality but what he believes her to be is only the product of his diseased imagination; actually she is one of the unforeseeing multitude. He himself joins the multitude and begins to decay; he is eventually saved, but because, on his return to generosity, he still demands what is unreal, he is destroyed.

The multitude of the unforeseeing is powerful in the novel. It includes Agnes Pembroke and her brother Herbert, who teaches Rickie practicality; and Rickie's aunt, his father's sister, the malignly witty and intelligent Mrs. Failing; and in the shadowy background the dreadful family on the shabby-genteel Silts; all these, in Shelley's words, "love not their fellow beings, live unfruitful lives and prepare for their old age a miserable grave."

Of Rickie it is said that "he suffered from the Primal Curse, which is not—as the Authorized Version suggests—the knowledge of good and evil, but the knowledge of good-and-evil." Yet at the same time he believes in absolutes. And it is easier, especially if one is weak, to act on absolutes than on a knowledge of good-and-evil. Rickie believes that he must choose between an absolute idealism and an absolute "practicality." Actually the choice is an unreal one, and five characters in the novel, three living and two dead, are never confronted with it. Rickie's mother and the manly sensitive farmer who loved her had known the way of love and instinct, and though chance had worked against them, they had been justified. Mr. Failing, the husband of Rickie's aunt, had chosen the way of love and intellect; a landowner, a member of Parliament, a political theorist, he had been loved by his tenants for the reforms on his estate (since undone by his widow) and his political wisdom had won him a small but worthy admiration.

The creation of the Failings is peculiarly brilliant, for Mrs. Failing is the false show and therefore the negation of what in her husband had been real. Intellectual and clever, she sees herself a romantic heroine of the mind; actually she has withered into a kind of fancy-picture of an 18th-century worldling, in "the habit of taking life with a laugh—as if life is a pill."

"I cannot stand smugness. It is the one, the unpardonable sin. Fresh air! . . . Even if it kills, I will let in the fresh air."

Thus reasoned Mrs. Failing in the facile vein of Ibsenism. She imagined herself to be a cold-eyed Scandinavian heroine. Really she was an old English lady, who did not mind giving other people a chill provided it was not infectious.

When we first see her she is engaged in chilling the memory of her dead husband, for as she writes the introduction to his posthumous essays, she subtly mocks his generosity. But that generosity had been large and wise.

Very notable was his distinction between coarseness and vulgarity (coarseness revealing something; vulgarity concealing something) and he showed an avowed preference for coarseness. Vulgarity, to him, had been the primal curse, the shoddy reticence that prevents man opening his heart to man, the power that makes against class equality. From it sprang all the things he hated—class shibboleths, ladies, lidies, the game laws, the Conservative party—all the things that accent the divergencies rather than the similarities in human nature.

"Attain the practical through the unpractical. There is no other road." Such had been Mr. Failing's belief and, together with a trust in the salutary powers of Nature and man, it puts him in the tradition of romanticism, of British liberal romanticism. Now, when romanticism is publicly mentioned only to explain its guilt in German ideology,[3] it is useful to remember Mr. Failing.

Stewart Ansell, Rickie's closest friend, is a kind of spiritual descendant of Mr. Failing. He is one of Forster's most successful characters. In *Aspects of the Novel* Forster speaks of two kinds of characters, "flat" and "round," but the distinction is neither original nor adequate, and does not properly describe Forster's own best creations. Like the appealing Ralph Touchett of Henry James's *Portrait of a Lady,* Ansell is neither flat nor round but *fragrant.*

More rigorously intellectual than Mr. Failing, Ansell is of the same stuff.

In many ways he was pedantic; but his pedantry lay close to the vineyards of life—far closer than that fetich Experience of the innumerable teacups.[4] He had a great many facts to learn, and before he died he learnt a suitable quantity. But he never forgot that the holiness of the heart's imagination can alone classify these facts—can alone decide which is an exception, which an example.

And when he sees the life of Rickie's boarding house at Sawston School, his comment is what Mr. Failing's would be:

"How unpractical it all is! . . . How unbusiness-like! They live together without love. They work without conviction. They seek money without requiring it. They die, and nothing will have happened, either

---

[3] Thus Mr. Herbert Agar, a poet, a scholar, and now a publicist, in his *A Time for Greatness,* a book based on romanticist ideas and infused with a romantic tone, blames (p. 65) modern German ideas on the romantic poets.

[4] Forster is not using the word "experience" in the sense in which it has been used earlier in this chapter. He means by it a prudent practicality; it is the teacup of experience that "has made men of Mr. Pembroke's type what they are." "Oh, that teacup! To be taken at prayers, at friendship, at love, till we are quite sane, efficient, quite experienced and quite useless to God or man. We must drink it, or we shall die. But we need not drink it always. Here is our problem and our salvation. There comes a moment—God knows when—at which we can say, 'I will experience no longer. I will create. I will be an experience.' But to do this we must be both acute and heroic. For it is not easy, after accepting six cups of tea, to throw the seventh in the face of the hostess."

for themselves or for others." It is a comment that the academic mind will often make when first confronted with the world.

Stewart Ansell is good in a way that Rickie cannot be—by his devotion to the intellect which makes him a whole person. The passionateness of his intelligence gives him his innocence and his insight. It is he who at first glance sees through Agnes, knows she is not there, or, if there, not a human person but a Medusa. It is he who precipitates the terrific scene in the dining-hall which is the novel's climax, making good his boast of the effectiveness of the intellectual. "When the moment comes," he had said, "I shall hit out like any ploughboy. Don't believe those lies about intellectual people. They're only written to soothe the majority."

No less than Ansell and more directly in the scheme of the novel, Stephen Wonham is descended from Mr. Failing. Stephen had, indeed, been Mr. Failing's protégé and now continues in the charge of Mrs. Failing. Apparently a great lout of a fellow, he has not been able to get on in the schools and so he lives on the Failing estate in Wiltshire, spending his time in the open with the tenants and laborers or reading third-rate agnostic pamphlets to understand the secrets of the universe. He is a Meredithian boy grown up, Crossjay Patterne some years older, and Mrs. Failing keeps him about as a kind of living literary symbol: he is the "fresh air"; she has little use for his honesty. Although a gentleman born, Stephen has none of the gentleman's attitude toward the poor, no notion of *noblesse oblige*. He will disgust Rickie by holding a personal grudge against a simple shepherd, just as he will disgust the intellectual Mrs. Failing because, when he lends money to his poor friends, he requires payment to the last farthing. He believes, in short, that his natural inferiors are his equals. He is vindictive and combative and affectionate; he is simple and trusting and, though slow, by no means stupid. Of him Stewart Ansell uses the word that Philip Herriton had used of Gino: he is "great."

Here then, in Mrs. Elliot and the man who loved her, in Mr. Failing, in Ansell and in Stephen, are people who choose the human way, neither being blasted by their own too high hopes nor sinking into torpor and decay. Rickie should have been of their number. Some fatality, some weakness, but most of all a wrong view of the nature of reality, drove him elsewhere, drove him to the plausible, practical Pembrokes and laid him open to the cruelty of Mrs. Failing.

Two kinds of people are counted among the unforeseeing multitude—those whose hearts are bad and those whose hearts are undeveloped. Among the former are Rickie's father and Rickie's aunt. Mrs. Failing is subtly aware of her condition and almost ashamed of it, but it has advantages. For if the good life "pays," so does the bad. It pays in different coin, but it pays—in the coin of power, superiority, possessions, or the pleasures of cruelty.

As for a man like Herbert Pembroke, he has the will to be good but the undeveloped heart prevents him. He is stupid. It is not clear whether his head diminishes his heart or his heart his head; in any case, some failure of connection between the two makes the stupidity.

What was amiss with Herbert? [Rickie] had known that something was amiss, and had entered the partnership with open eyes. The man was kind and unselfish; more than that, he was truly charitable, and it was a real pleasure to him to give pleasure to others. Certainly he might talk too much about it afterwards; but it was the doing, not the talking, that he really valued, and benefactors of this sort are not too common. He was, moreover, diligent and conscientious: his heart was in his work, and his adherence to the Church of England no mere matter of form. He was capable of affection: he was usually courteous and tolerant. Then what was amiss? Why, in spite of all these qualities, should Rickie feel that there was something wrong with him—nay, that he was wrong as a whole, and that if the Spirit of Humanity should ever hold a judgment he would assuredly be classed among the goats?[5] The answer at first sight appeared a graceless one—it was that Herbert was stupid. Not stupid in the ordinary sense—he had a businesslike brain, and acquired knowledge easily—but stupid in the important sense: his whole life was coloured by a contempt of the intellect. That he had a tolerable intellect of his own was not the point: it is in what we value, not in what we have, that the test of us resides.

[5] See page 83 for a discussion of goats.

Herbert was Sawston and Sawston School, genteel and cultivated philistinism, very full of "ideals," and when Rickie married Herbert's sister, he became a part of Sawston—for "practical" reasons. The marriage with Agnes was based on an illusion which each of the parties entertained, a falsification of reality. For poor Rickie, the illusion was of Agnes's sexual and moral warmth. What shone about her was no quality of her own, or anything he could stimulate her to; it was what had been generated by Gerald and herself in the passionate kiss Rickie had witnessed—but "she was never to be so real to him again."

Indeed, although the novelist does not say so, we can almost imagine that Rickie was in love not so much with the girl herself as with her "manly" and brutal lover, in love in the sense that he was identifying himself with the strong and dominant man by marrying this "girl like an empress," this "kindly Medea, a Cleopatra with a sense of duty"; Agnes, with her gay talk of horsewhipping, her pleasure at the idea of the weak boy in the hands of the strong boy, was Gerald's counterpart.

As for Agnes, apart from the convenience of the marriage, she had been dazzled by Rickie's single moment of spiritual power. For Gerald died—in the most notable of the sudden deaths: Chapter V begins, "Gerald died that afternoon. He was broken up in the football match"—and Agnes had prepared to meet the terrible blow with fortitude and phlegm. But Rickie forces her to "mind" the tragedy.

> "It's the worst thing that can ever happen to you in all your life, and you've got to mind it—you've got to mind it. They'll come saying, 'Bear up—trust to time.' No, no; they're wrong. Mind it. . . . It's your death as well as his. He's gone, Agnes, and his arms will never hold you again. In God's name, mind such a thing, and don't sit fencing with your soul. Don't stop being great; that's the one crime he'll never forgive you."

Agnes "minds" and is "great": it is her one moment of greatness. Neither she nor Rickie is great again. Agnes is conventional, snobbish, hard. Rickie is second-best for her; he cannot continue to arouse her imagination by his insight and certainly not by his sexuality. She must be dominated or dominating, and her notion of dominance is mixed up with some notion of brutality. She is not dominated, therefore she becomes dominant and thus she deteriorates. We move into a new moral dimension with this situation, for Agnes, Forster points out, is helped toward her deterioration by Rickie's very virtues which kept him from mastery.

"If I had a girl, I'd keep her in line," is not the remark of a fool nor of a cad.[6] Rickie had not kept his wife in line. He had shown her all the workings of his soul, mistaking this for love; and in consequence she was the worse woman after two years of marriage . . .

Rickie, drawn by the exigencies of his marriage into the life of Sawston School, takes to "practicality" with a vengeance, and is ruined by it. He does nothing very bad, only petty little things in the interests of quite legitimate sums of money, things which he is almost proud to do because they seem to him mature and better than his old college notions. But he becomes a martinet in class and a cat's-paw in Herbert's dull, sullen war on the day-boys. What happens to him is nothing spectacular. It is only that a "cloud of unreality" settles upon his spirit.

The cloud had not been made by Sawston School and it had been of his own choosing, though Agnes had directed the choice. He had chosen it just before his marriage when he and Agnes had gone to visit Mrs. Failing in Wiltshire. There for the first time he had met Stephen Wonham. They had ridden to Salisbury Cathedral together, disliking each other and showing their dislike, Rickie by acting like a prig, Stephen by acting like a boor; Stephen had culminated his boorishness by getting drunk and singing an obscene song about Mrs. Failing.

And then it turns out that this boisterous and disgusting young man is Rickie's half-brother: the casual communication of this fact is Mrs. Failing's revenge upon Rickie after a small difference of opinion. The news shatters Rickie rather more than Mrs. Failing had expected. He is convinced that Stephen is bad with all his

---

[6] The remark had been made by Stephen Wonham and it is referred to at the close of the story when we get a glimpse of Stephen's marriage.

father's badness. Yet he feels he must claim the kinship; Stephen must know of their brotherhood. "Why?" says Agnes.

"Because he must be told such a real thing."
"Such a real thing?" the girl echoed, screwing up her forehead. "But you don't mean you're glad about it?"
His head bowed down over the letter. "My God—no! But it's a real thing . . ."

Yet actually, to Rickie, Stephen is merely a moral symbol, not a real person. Love can degenerate as well as regenerate a man and Rickie, unaware "how slovenly his own perceptions had been during the past week, how dogmatic and intolerant his attitude to all that was not Love," allows Agnes to have her way and keeps quiet the matter of his relation to Stephen. The half-brothers separate without Stephen knowing the "real thing."

Thus the cloud of unreality settles down upon Rickie, deepening as Sawston claims him more and more, Cambridge and his friends less and less. Ansell refuses to see this painfully deteriorated friend and Rickie stands alone, his marriage quite dead, his self a burden to him. A daughter born with more than the usual Elliot deformity dies mercifully soon.

Rickie's release comes by chance and melodrama—by Ansell and Stephen meeting on his lawn, and by a revelation. Stephen and Ansell begin their acquaintance with a fight. The reason for the fight is absurd, they act like a pair of small boys: it simply suits Forster to have the head and the heart engage in a physical struggle before they become, as they do, fast friends. They become friends over Mr. Failing; Ansell is reading and admiring his book, Stephen had known the living man. Only one conversation between Stephen and Mr. Failing is recorded.

Years ago, when a nurse was washing [Stephen], he had slipped from her soapy hands and had got up [to the roof of the mansion]. She implored him to remember that he was a little gentleman; but he forgot the fact—if it was a fact—and not even the butler could get him down. Mr. Failing who was sitting alone in the garden too ill to read, heard a shout. "Am I an acroterium?" He looked up and saw a naked child poised on the summit of Cadover. "Yes," he replied; "but they are unfashionable. Go in," and the vision had remained with him as something peculiarly gracious. He felt that nonsense and beauty have close connections,—closer connections than Art will allow,—and that both would remain when his own heaviness and ugliness had perished. Mrs. Failing found in his remains a sentence that puzzled her. "I see the respectable mansion. I see the smug fortress of culture. The doors are shut. The windows are shut. But on the roof the children go dancing for ever."

But Stephen is no longer on the roof of the mansion and the doors and windows are shut against him—he has been turned out of Cadover by Mrs. Failing. He has ceased to amuse; and he has angered her by making the tenants and laborers restless and telling them what their rights are. He has made a fuss about a dangerous railroad crossing that has already played a part in the story and will again, and Agnes has seen to it that an account of the ribald song should reach the ears of Mrs. Failing. So, refusing to accept money from his benefactress, accepting only a packet of old letters, he has come hungry and penniless to tell Rickie that he has learned they are half-brothers. To Ansell, Stephen is "wonderful" as Gino had been to Caroline and Philip.

He was not romantic, for Romance is a figure with outstretched hands, yearning for the unattainable. Certain figures of the Greeks, to whom we continually return, suggested him a little. One expected nothing of him—no purity of phrase nor swift edged thought. Yet the conviction grew that he had been back somewhere—back to some table of the gods, spread in a field where there is no noise, and that he belonged for ever to the guests with whom he had eaten.

Meanwhile he was simple and frank, and what he could tell he would tell any one. He had not the suburban reticence.

What he tells is that he has discovered that Rickie and he had the same mother. This news comes to Rickie himself in an impossible and rather superb scene, whose truth, as Peter Burra says, is "operatic." Ansell reveals the great fact in a furious denunciation of Rickie before the whole boarding-house of boys assembled for dinner: he is justly indignant, for Agnes has just tried to buy off Stephen from claiming brotherhood and Rickie has refused to ac-

knowledge a wicked brother who is the by-blow of his father's wick-
edness. The revelation of the truth is to Rickie a terrible shock, yet
he recovers quickly from it and when, some days later, Stephen returns, roaring drunk and vindictive, and sets to smashing up the
house, Rickie has gone through a crisis in his emotions which has
made him ready for brotherhood. He offers to help Stephen and to
"cure" him, but Stephen knows that the offer is a merely principled
one, made from Rickie's idealization of their mother, not from any
feeling for him. In the end, it is Rickie who is cured by Stephen's
inducing him to leave Agnes, Dunwood House and Sawston.

But Rickie is still to be destroyed. As the novel approaches its
close, it moves with a certain ambiguousness, yet its point is clear.
The illusion of Agnes has been exorcised but a new illusion takes
its place—Rickie has begun to see his mother's spirit in his newly
discovered brother, assuming a moral quality in him which is not
in fact there. Once again the illustrious superstition begins to work
in Rickie. Stephen has been drinking heavily, Rickie is much dis-
tressed and at last manages to elicit a promise of sobriety. But
Stephen breaks the promise and Rickie is devastated—he is, as he
says, bankrupt for the second time. Under the spell of his noble
superstition he is quite blind to the simple reality of a drunken
man; all he can see is that his mother's spirit is being defiled: "the
woman he loved would die out, in drunkenness, in debauchery, and
her strength would be dissipated by a man, her beauty defiled by a
man. She would not continue." And for Rickie this fantastic notion
of his mother's destruction means that he must return to Agnes and
be corrupted by her.

He had just come from a conversation with Mrs. Failing; she had
told him to go back to Agnes, to trust to conventions and to beware
of the earth, and now he cries, "May God receive and pardon me
for trusting the earth." He is with his aunt's butler, Leighton, a
simple man who understands that Stephen is simply drunk, and the
simple man says, "But, Mr. Elliot, what have you done that's
wrong?" Rickie answers, "Gone bankrupt, Leighton, for the second time. Pretended again that people are real. May God have

mercy on me!" The judgment comes at once: "Leighton dropped his arm. Though he did not understand, a chill of disgust passed over him . . ." For Leighton knows that people are real.

And now Rickie, looking for the drunken Stephen, finds him lying stupefied on the railroad tracks as an engine approaches. He saves Stephen but has no desire to save himself.

Wearily he did a man's duty. There was time to raise him up and push him to safety. It is also a man's duty to save his own life, and therefore he tried. The train went over his knees. He died up in Cadover, whispering, "You have been right," to Mrs. Failing.

Thus had Rickie destroyed himself by mistaking the nature of reality. Had he been able to conceive Stephen's personal existence, not merely his ideal existence, he would not have been, in Shelley's words, "blasted by his disappointment," nor descended to an "untimely grave."

Yet Rickie is justified and the "earth" is justified. Some part of Rickie will survive in the mythological stories he has written—readers of *The Celestial Omnibus* will recognize them as actually Forster's own; in the coda with which the novel ends Herbert Pembroke dickers with Stephen over the rights and royalties they are to share. But Rickie's justification is fullest in Stephen. To Rickie Stephen owes not only his physical but his spiritual life, his salvation in happiness and responsiveness, in his farm, wife and child. The last note of the story is the theme of Rickie's survival; Stephen, to acknowledge his gratitude to Rickie in the best way he knows, "bent down reverently and saluted [his] child; to whom he had given the name of their mother." The generous error and noble superstition had destroyed Rickie himself (as it had destroyed Shelley with his ever-intensifying search for death) but it had saved others, for although erroneous it was generous, and though superstitious it was noble, and it asserted, foolishly but firmly, the real existence of things.

CHAPTER SIX

A Room with a View

IN ORDER of publication, *A Room with a View,* which appeared in 1908, is the third of Forster's novels. But in order of conception it may perhaps have been the first, for Forster drafted a large part of it in 1903. Certainly in the Italian setting of its early scenes and in the manner of its comedy, its affinities are with *Where Angels Fear to Tread* rather than with *The Longest Journey.* In scale and tone it is even smaller and lighter than *Where Angels Fear to Tread,* its manner is airier, it takes more color from the outdoors and more charm from human absurdity, and the quality of its comedy is more romantic; but the comedy is also shot through with a sense of melodramatic evil which, though not so violently expressed as that of the first Italian comedy, is more frightening in its gratuitousness and in its restraint.

Comedy, we are often told, depends on incongruity. We are less often told that tragedy has the same dependence. The incongruity is between the real and the unreal; both comedy and tragedy require blind characters. In *Oedipus Rex* and *King Lear* the blindness finds physical expression; in *Othello* the many metaphors of vision stress Othello's inability to see what is before his eyes, and Orgon in *Tartuffe* is as unable as Othello to see what his senses present to him. This confusion of the real with the unreal, which had touched

Forster's first novel and dominated his second, is also the theme of *A Room with a View*.

The incongruity on which the comedy of the novel rests is symbolized by the blood on certain photographs. They are Alinari prints of some of the famous pictures of Florence and have been bought by Lucy Honeychurch, an excessively proper though quite pretty girl, who is traveling in Italy with her elderly cousin, Charlotte Bartlett. The purpose of the photographs is to remind Lucy, when she returns to England, of her triumphant appreciation of Giotto's tactile values. But in the Piazza Signoria, at "the hour of unreality—the hour, that is, when unfamiliar things are real," two men, Florentines, argue about money and one draws a knife and stabs the other; Lucy faints into the arms of young George Emerson, a fellow guest at her pension, and as George escorts her home, he throws a little package into the Arno—it is her photographs, he explains, which have been stained with the blood of the murdered man.

For Mr. Eager, an English clergyman resident in Florence, the event in the Piazza is a disgrace to the fair traditional city. "This very square—so I am told—witnessed yesterday the most sordid of tragedies. To one who loves the Florence of Dante and Savonarola there is something portentous in such desecration—portentous and humiliating." The irony is almost too obvious. Mr. Eager, choosing to forget what the Florence of Dante and Savonarola was like, has turned life into art; thus it can be contemplated by the timid. But art is not life, as we are reminded by the blood that now and then falls on our pictures, or to be more precise, we should say that the art of the timid is not life: to the courageous the pictures have had blood on them from the first.

Caroline Abbott had said "I mean it crudely—you know what I mean. . . . Get over supposing I'm refined," and *A Room with a View* is about "crudeness" and "refinement." Its theme is stated by the old socialist, Mr. Emerson: "Love is of the body—not the body, but of the body." It deals with the physical reality upon which all the other realities rest. The blindness to this reality is the source of the comedy and the comedy is played out to the verge of tragedy.

The blood on the photographs is symbolic not only of the novel's point but also of its method. Nothing could be more artful, nothing more disembodied than this story about naturalness and the body. Its hero and heroine are as nearly creatures of air or mythology as it is possible for two young people to be in a story about sexuality. As in any good novel, the characters grow out of the author's prose, and the prose of *A Room with a View* is swift and airy, its most memorable effects are of impalpability, of brightness and of wind. At the very end of the book darkness and evil are introduced, and for the first time we see that we have, after all, been dealing with matters of great consequence and reality. The effect of the contrast, of the sudden introduction of evil into what has seemed an almost trivial world, is remarkable—almost too remarkable: we feel that a novel should not acquire its stature from a single effect.

The slender story begins with a room without a view. Lucy and Charlotte, when they had first arrived at the Pension Bertolini, were sorely disappointed in their rooms which, contrary to promise, had no view. Old Mr. Emerson, publicly and loudly, but in all generosity, had offered to exchange rooms, for his and his son's did have views. We must suppose for this novel a state of manners which permits Miss Honeychurch and Miss Bartlett to be embarrassed and even affronted by the offer and to refuse it, although perhaps such manners are archaic even for 1908; it is not until Mr. Beebe, a clergyman of their acquaintance, assures them of the propriety of accepting the offer that they consent to make the exchange. But they continue to be as cool as possible to the Emersons.

Both George and Lucy are young people imprisoned, Lucy by her respectability, George by a deep, neurotic *fin de siècle* pessimism. But the scene of death on the Piazza has not been lost upon them. It begins, indeed, the destruction of their prisons. George has held Lucy in his arms and now wants to live. Lucy's dull propriety begins to give way before the possibility of passion.

As a matter of fact, Mr. Beebe has been wondering about Lucy ever since he heard her rather startling performance of Beethoven. Suddenly—and irritably—she begins to develop. She has come to Florence for "culture"—for correct knowledge about Giotto's tactile values and to buy "florid little picture frames that seemed fashioned in gilt pastry; other little frames, more severe, that stood on little easels and were carven out of oak; a blotting book of vellum; a Dante of the same material; cheap brooches, . . . pins, pots, heraldic saucers, brown art-photographs; Eros and Psyche in alabaster, St. Peter to match," all the facile tourist-trove of phrases and objects. And she finds instead "the eternal league of Italy with youth." She discovers that she has less respect for Charlotte, for Mr. Eager, even for Miss Eleanora Lavish, the novelist who is so free and frank, who tells her that "one doesn't come to Italy for niceness, one comes for life," and who is quite sure that life is local color.

Then on a picnic there is some confusion and Lucy, in search of the two clergymen, asks the coachman in her limited Italian, "Dove buoni uomini?" The coachman, having his own notion of what a good man is, directs her to George Emerson. She tumbles down a bank to a flowery terrace, and the flowers, the sudden wide vista of the Val d'Arno and her own emotions quite overcome her and she submits to George's kiss. But before a word can be exchanged between them the "silence of life had been broken by Miss Bartlett who stood brown against the view."

George's is the first of three kisses by which the comedy is punctuated. Lucy receives the next one from a young man named Cecil Vyse. For Lucy, confused by her own passion, has submitted to the wisdom of the brown Charlotte Bartlett. Old Mr. Emerson had declared at the picnic that Lorenzo de Medici had been quite right when he said, "Don't go fighting against the spring," but Charlotte knew how to wage just that fight. Convinced herself, she convinces Lucy that George, like all men, is a rake and his kiss but a masculine "exploit." "Do you remember that day at lunch when he argued with Miss Alan that liking one person is an extra reason for liking another?" Charlotte says to prove her point.[1] She is an artist in precaution; the world she has contrived and now presents to Lucy is a "cheerless, loveless world in which the young rush to destruction until they learn better—a shamefaced world of precautions and barriers. . . ." Later, in *Howards End*, Forster comments at some length on the tragedy of precaution:

Actual life is full of false clues and sign-posts that lead nowhere. With infinite effort we nerve ourselves for a crisis that never comes. The most successful career must show a waste of strength that might have moved mountains, and the most unsuccessful is not that of a man who is taken unprepared, but of him who has prepared and is never taken. On a tragedy of that kind our national morality is duly silent. It assumes that preparation against danger is itself a good, and that men, like nations, are the better for staggering through life fully armed. The tragedy of preparedness has scarcely been handled, save by the Greeks. Life is indeed dangerous, but not in the way morality would have us believe. It is indeed unmanageable, but the essence of it is not a battle. It is unmanageable because it is a romance, and its essence romantic beauty.

But Charlotte knows otherwise and carries Lucy off to Rome where Cecil Vyse is staying (with his mother); Cecil falls in love with Lucy from the heights of a clearly superior culture and later, in England, Lucy accepts his offer of marriage. The engagement is not the occasion for Cecil's kiss. The kiss does not occur until some days later, a delay which has been criticized (by Miss Rose Macaulay in her book on Forster) as unnatural, as no doubt it is. But unnaturalness, even to this extreme, is part of Cecil's nature and the story is now for some time to be preoccupied with Cecil's nature. It

---

[1] *Epipsychidion* is again relevant:

> Love is like understanding, that grows bright,
> Gazing on many truths; 'tis like thy light,
> Imagination! which from earth and sky,
> And from the depths of human fantasy,
> As from a thousand prisms and mirrors, fills
> The Universe with glorious beams, and kills
> Error, the worm, with many a sun-like arrow
> Of its reverberated lightning. Narrow
> The heart that loves, the brain that contemplates,
> The life that wears, the spirit that creates
> One object, and one form, and builds thereby
> A sepulchre for its eternity.

becomes Meredithian—in the social comedy that ensues, in the praise of Nature and naturalness, in Lucy's young brother Freddy with his true perceptions, in the scene of sunshine and water that is to be the second meeting of George and Lucy, and most of all in the dissection of Cecil.

For Cecil is a small Willoughby Patterne and Lucy is his Clara Middleton to be shaped to his notion of what an advanced young woman should be. Forster, however, is more generous than Meredith in whose pursuit of Sir Willoughby there is something almost madly obsessive and entirely cruel; in *The Egoist,* comedy's "slim, feasting smile" (a phrase which always suggests the merrier grave-worms) becomes almost the baying of hounds. Forster's relation to the Meredithian spirit is complex; as he tells us in *Aspects of the Novel,* Meredith had meant much to him in his youth, as to all emancipated young people in the early years of the century; yet even as he uses the Meredithian spirit he dissociates himself from it by making Cecil himself a devotee of Meredithian comedy.

Freddy Honeychurch begins the dissection. He does not like Cecil, he cannot understand why.

Cecil praised one too much for being athletic. Was that it? Cecil made one talk in one's own way. This tired one. Was that it? And Cecil was the kind of fellow who would never wear another fellow's cap. Unaware of his own profundity, Freddy checked himself. He must be jealous, or he would not dislike a man for such foolish reasons.

And the novelist takes the matter up where Freddy leaves off.

Appearing thus late in the story, Cecil must be at once described. He was medieval. Like a Gothic statue. Tall and refined, with shoulders that seemed braced square by an effort of will, and a head that was tilted a little higher than the usual level of vision, he resembled those fastidious saints who guard the portals of a French cathedral. Well educated, well endowed and not deficient physically, he remained in the grip of a certain devil whom the modern world knows as self-consciousness, and whom the medieval, with dimmer vision, worshipped as asceticism. A Gothic statue implies celibacy, just as a Greek statue implies fruition. . . . And Freddy, who ignored history and art, perhaps meant the same when he failed to imagine Cecil wearing another fellow's cap.

Cecil despises women who talk about cookery and he has a quick eye for interior decoration; he is the cultured man in this story and although he is not cruel, like Rickie Elliot's father, his culture makes him peevish and superior. Culture for him is a way of hiding his embarrassment before life. He is taken to call on Lucy's mother's old friends and, feeling the engaged man's natural resentment, he behaves badly. Certainly it had been a bore, "yet the smirking old women, however wrong individually, were racially correct," and Cecil should have had wit enough to see it.

The comedy now proceeds on good-and-bad taste. A certain Mr. Flack, a contractor, has built two villas which horrify the gentry of the neighborhood. They are very ugly, but, as usual, Forster is on the side of ugly houses. If Mr. Flack is not properly trained in the use of columns, still his columns, bad as their capitals are, represent Mr. Flack's own taste and desire. Sir Harry Otway, the leader of local society, had vainly tried to direct Mr. Flack's taste; now he has bought the villas, meaning to tear them down, only to find that Mr. Flack has installed an aged, bed-ridden aunt in one of them. How to let the other is a problem, for it is too expensive for the peasant class and too small and dreadful for "any one the least like us." It is a house for a bank clerk and everyone fears that a bank clerk will rent it. But Cecil, the devotee of Meredithian comedy (he possessed, in addition, "his full share of medieval mischievousness"), solves the problem of the tenant. He has struck up an acquaintance with the Emersons in London and he thinks it a fine stroke to introduce this strange pair to the community.

But before this has happened, Lucy had been kissed by Cecil. He has noticed that when Lucy walks with him she sticks to the road and avoids the fields and trees. He comments on this and she agrees it is so; indeed, when he questions her further, she says that she thinks of him always as in a room—a drawing room and without a view. But she is good-naturedly willing to walk in the woods with him; and beside a tiny pool that sometimes fills up in a heavy rain, she is quite willing to be kissed. It is not a successful kiss except as it reminds Lucy of George's.

The comedy begins to be played out quickly and in the open. With the Emersons coming to the villa, Lucy is in a panic and reproaches Cecil for his trick; he, thinking she is snobbish—snobs in Forster's novels always think everybody else is snobbish—and planning to educate her in the best ideas, tells her, "I believe in democracy," and is surprised to hear her snap, "No you don't. You don't know what the word means." More is involved in this little love story than love; as always in Forster, sexuality and right political feeling have a point of contact.

George and Lucy meet again. It is just after George has been swimming with Freddy and Mr. Beebe in the pool, and the pool in the sun and wind "had been a call to the blood and the relaxed will" and had dispelled his bleak neurotic despair. He runs shouting through the woods and comes face to face with Lucy and Mrs. Honeychurch, neither of whom is quite shocked at his being, except for Mr. Beebe's clerical hat, quite naked. The mischief is done and George's exhilaration—and Lucy's—continues on the tennis-court.

He wanted to live now, to win at tennis, to stand for all he was worth in the sun—in the sun which had begun to decline and was shining in her eyes; and he did win.

* * * * *

He jumped over the net and sat down at her feet, asking: "You—are you tired?"
"Of course I'm not!"
"Do you mind being beaten?"
She was going to answer "No," when it struck her that she did mind, so she answered, "Yes."

And it is because of Cecil's behavior about tennis that Lucy finally jilts him. She hears Freddy begging Cecil to make a fourth at tennis and Cecil's voice replying.

"My dear Freddy, I am no athlete. As you well remarked this very morning, 'There are some chaps who are no good for anything except books'; I plead guilty to being such a chap, and will not inflict myself on you."
The scales fell from Lucy's eyes. How had she stood Cecil for a mo-

ment? It was absolutely intolerable, and the same evening she broke off her engagement.

Cecil jilted is a better man than Cecil engaged; "for all his culture, Cecil was an ascetic at heart and nothing in his love became him like the leaving of it." But Lucy's break with Cecil does not mean her union with George. He has caught her behind a bush and kissed her again; and she knows that his first kiss was not an "exploit," but again she turns to Charlotte Bartlett and, for no reason, refuses to marry George. It is here that the story passes into strangeness and into something like horror. It passes, indeed, from Lucy and George to two other people. They are Miss Bartlett and Mr. Beebe.

As the story makes this change, Lucy stands on the brink of an abyss. Charlotte Bartlett's words of congratulation are the first Lucy hears when she refuses George and she responds to them with the pert and vulgar words of her own self-congratulation; her voice rings with Charlotte's favorite manner. As she goes out of doors, she is "aware of autumn"—"summer was ending and the evening brought her odours of decay, the more pathetic because they were reminiscent of spring." In the subtle—sometimes too subtle—thematic fashion he often uses, Forster had written almost these very words earlier in the novel when he had said of the sweet elderly Miss Alan of the Pension Bertolini that "A delicate pathos perfumed her disconnected remarks, giving them unexpected beauty, just as in the decaying autumn woods there sometimes arise odours reminiscent of spring."

Now Miss Alan and her sister—they have touched the story lightly again as possible tenants for the Flack villa—are on the point of another tour, this time to Greece and the near East; they want the name of "a really comfortable pension in Constantinople." And they beckon Lucy—not only to the trip but to the state of being a Miss Alan. Charlotte Bartlett also beckons. Something deep in Lucy wants to follow. She wants to join the "unforeseeing multitude" of *Alastor* which is the same as the "vast armies of the benighted" to which Charlotte is recruiting her.

It did not do to think, nor, for the matter of that, to feel. She gave up trying to understand herself, and joined the vast armies of the benighted, who follow neither the heart nor the brain, and march to their destiny by catch-words. The armies are full of pleasant and pious folk. But they have yielded to the only enemy that matters—the enemy within. They have sinned against passion and truth, and vain will be their strife after virtue. As the years pass, they are censured. Their pleasantry and their piety show cracks, their wit becomes cynicism, their unselfishness hypocrisy; they feel and produce discomfort wherever they go. They have sinned against Eros and against Pallas Athene, and not by any heavenly intervention, but by the ordinary course of nature, those allied deities will be avenged.

Lucy entered this army when she pretended to George that she did not love him, and pretended to Cecil that she loved no one. The night received her, as it had received Miss Bartlett thirty years before.

And of this Mr. Beebe is glad. The sunny comedy had darkened with Lucy's response to the temptation of celibacy; it becomes terrifying with Mr. Beebe's happiness at Lucy's sure movement toward the benighted army. The effect of surprise is almost illegitimate. ". . . Who would have supposed," we have been asked of Mr. Beebe early in the story, "that tolerance, sympathy, and a sense of humour would inhabit that militant form?" And when the tolerant Mr. Beebe had seemed disappointed over the engagement of Cecil and Lucy, could it be anything but dissatisfaction on the part of one who understood the implication of the way Lucy played Beethoven? And this seemed surely to account, too, for his pleasure when the engagement was broken. Yet now—

His belief in celibacy, so reticent, so carefully concealed beneath his tolerance and culture, now came to the surface and expanded like some delicate flower. "They that marry do well, but they that refrain do better." So ran his belief, and he never heard that an engagement was broken off but with a slight feeling of pleasure. In the case of Lucy, the feeling was intensified through dislike of Cecil: and he was willing to go further—to place her out of danger until she could confirm her resolution of virginity. The feeling was very subtle and quite undogmatic, and he never imparted it to any other of the characters in this entanglement. Yet it existed, and it alone explains his action subsequently, and his influence on the action of others. The compact that he made with Miss Bartlett in the tavern, was to help not only Lucy, but religion also.

The feeling against religion in this novel is naive and direct and makes a small sub-plot. In Florence Mr. Eager—he had been carefully contrasted with Mr. Beebe but now we know that both are cut from the same cloth—had hinted that old Mr. Emerson had, in effect, murdered his wife, George's mother. But we learn that Mr. Eager himself had been the "murderer" of Mrs. Emerson, for when George had had typhoid in childhood, Mr. Eager had played upon Mrs. Emerson's fears about her son's lack of baptism—"he made her think about sin, and she went under thinking about it." And now Mr. Beebe is trying to murder Lucy's soul.

But help comes from an unexpected source. Lucy moves more and more to Charlotte Bartlett until even her mother comments on the resemblance in tone, but it is Charlotte Bartlett who rescues Lucy by bringing her face to face, in Mr. Beebe's study, with old Mr. Emerson. Mr. Beebe had not wanted them to meet and he is furious with Miss Bartlett, knowing that Mr. Emerson could win the day for his son. And in this scene the old agnostic has "the face of a saint who understood," while at the news of Lucy's surrender to George, Mr. Beebe's face is "suddenly inhuman." To him the whole affair is "lamentable, lamentable—incredible." He can never forgive the young people.

Together on their honeymoon at the Pension Bertolini, George and Lucy try to puzzle out Miss Bartlett's reversal. That she knew Mr. Emerson was in the study is certain. Then why had she brought Lucy to the study? Something deeper than her deep negation had wished the right outcome of the affair, just as something beneath Mr. Beebe's warm tolerance wanted it killed.

[George] whispered: ". . . I'll put a marvel to you. That your cousin always hoped. That from the very first moment we met, she hoped, far down in her mind, that we should be like this—of course very far down. That she fought us on the surface, and yet she hoped. I can't explain her any other way. Can you? Look how she kept me alive in you all the summer; how she gave you no peace; how month after month she became more eccentric and unreliable. The sight of us haunted her—or she couldn't have described us as she did to her friend [Miss Lavish.] There are details—it burnt. I read the book afterwards. She is not frozen, Lucy, she is not withered up all through. She tore us apart twice, but in the rectory that evening she was given one more chance to make us happy. We can never make friends with her or thank her. But I do believe that, far down in her heart, far below all speech and behaviour, she is glad."

"It is impossible," murmured Lucy, and then, remembering the experiences of her own heart, she said: "No—it is just possible."

As Forster sees the mind, such are its depths and contradictions.

The occasion for Mr. Montgomery Belgion's essay, "The Diabolism of E. M. Forster" was Mr. Belgion's perception that Forster divides mankind into sheep and goats and has no pity on the goats. "For Mr. Forster, it seems evident, you are either born a sheep or a goat, and, whichever it is, that you are doomed to remain. There is no hope for you." And Mr. Belgion continues: ". . . For that great mass of unfortunate outsiders Mr. Forster has no pity. . . . On the contrary,—and here we reach a very significant thing, it seems to me —on the contrary, he sneers at them." Had Mr. Belgion been less doctrinally elated over his discovery and had he not overstated his case with oddly bitter talk about "mockery" and "sneering" and "a smell of brimstone," he might have reported accurately what does happen in Forster's novel. For the fact is that in Forster there is a deep and important irresolution over the question of whether the world is one of good and evil, sheep and goats, or one of good-and-evil, of sheep who are somehow goats and goats who are somehow sheep. In *A Room with a View* he compromises—as it is the novelist's right to compromise—between these two views. Mr. Beebe is goat, Charlotte is goat with a sheep somehow hidden within her, she is good-and-evil. And this uncertainty about moral judgment will haunt Forster's intellectual life; on the whole, the view which sees life as good-and-evil will gain over the other, but it will never be completely in control.

CHAPTER SEVEN

Howards End

BIOGRAPHY intrudes itself into literary judgment and keeps it from being "pure." As we form our opinion of a particular work, certainly the sole object of our thought should be the work itself. But it seldom is—and although we call extraneous the facts that thrust themselves upon us, they inevitably enter into our judgment. We are always conscious of an author, and this consciousness does not rise only from elements in the work; the extraneous personal facts that reach us are never wholly ignored. Literary facts are as intrusive as personal facts, though no doubt they are more "legitimate." The author's whole career presents itself to us not improperly as an architectonic whole of which each particular work is a part; and the shape of that career, the nature and pace of its development, the past failures and successes or those which we know are to come, the very size of the structure, the place of any single unit in the logic of the whole—all bear upon our feelings about any particular work.

In reading Forster there are two literary facts that affect us. One is that, despite an early fecundity which produced four remarkable novels in five years, Forster waited fourteen years to produce his fifth, after which he produced nothing for an even longer period. Perhaps his future biographer will be able to explain his temporary

retirement between 1910, the year of *Howards End*, and 1924, the
year of *A Passage to India*, and the second and possibly permanent
retirement after the great success of this last novel. But even unex-
plained, the facts suggest an unusual relation of a man to his craft.
In our feeling about Henry James, for instance, it is an element,
with a meaning which could no doubt be expressed, that his production is so very large; and we find a similarly implicit significance
in the fact that Stendhal waited until he was forty-eight to produce
the first of his great novels and until he was fifty-six to produce the
second. Just so, it intrudes upon us as an important element in our
feeling about Forster that, having mastered his art, he has twice
abandoned it. No doubt, with some difficulty, that feeling could be
made precise; it fluctuates between disapproval of a dereliction from
duty and a sense of relief that a fine artist has not seen art as a grim
imperative.

The other literary fact that is likely to influence our feelings about
all of Forster's novels is that they are by the author of *Howards
End*. This is not to imply a denigration of the other work or to
suggest a significant difference in quality. But *Howards End* is
undoubtedly Forster's masterpiece; it develops to their full the
themes and attitudes of the early books and throws back upon them
a new and enhancing light. It justifies these attitudes by connecting
them with a more mature sense of responsibility.

For when we have emerged from the immediate seduction of
Where Angels Fear to Tread, The Longest Journey and *A Room
with a View* we can sometimes feel that their assumptions have
been right but rather too easy. In one disguise or another, the mythology and fantasy of the early stories have found their way into the
novels, and the mythology formulates well but abstractly, the fantasy
solves dashingly but sometimes facilely. The formulations and the
solutions have been just, but they have not been worked out against
sufficient resistance. We have learned that naturalness is to be trusted,
that authority and society are stupid and insincere. But we have
learned this in a mythologcial way, as if by parable, and with a great

deal of attractive *brio* and *bravura;* we have not seen it put to the test. In the early novels what is bad in life has indeed the look of reality, but what is good has the appearance of myth.

Forster is wonderfully accurate in his perception of the failures in human relationships and he accurately names causes. But although the true relationships he sets up against the false do indeed adequately illuminate badness, they are never in themselves real. Thus Gino can stand as a criticism of English feeling, but he cannot be part of Caroline's life. Agnes and Mrs. Failing are entirely alive, but Rickie's mother, the symbol of life, is dead and a spirit; and although Stephen marries happily we never see his wife, she is only a voice. It is certainly significant that although we hear much about the transcendent values of sexual love, we are never shown a happy marriage, and when we consider the importance of Ansell in *The Longest Journey* we cannot ignore the weight of his condemnation of marriage.[1] Lucy and George, we feel, are too impalpable for anything but a merely symbolic union.

Then too, we can become a little weary of Forster's way of dealing with authority. I. A. Richards speaks of Forster's hatred of doctors, schoolmasters and clergymen; they are the representatives of authority and always stupid and insincere. Mr. Richards is mistaken when he says that Forster's "real audience is youth, caught at that stage when rebellion against the uncomfortable conventions is easy because the cost of abandoning them has not been fully counted." Forster's real audience is maturity, but Mr. Richards has located the element which might possibly alienate mature people.

The attack on authority is not itself a fault, it may even be a virtue; but it requires some equally forceful indication of what *right* authority should be. For example, Mr. Fielding of *A Passage to India* is the single example of a responsible man who is admirable, but significantly he is admirable only so long as he rather despises the job he does so well; when he takes it seriously he is less to be

---

[1] On the other hand, Rickie, in his moment of regeneration, asserts that happy marriages are possible. But his statement is not nearly so passionate as Ansell's aphorisms on the deep incompatibility of men and women.

trusted. Again, although the emotion of parenthood has been so important in the novels, it is never adequately represented beyond its lyric expression. With the exception of Mr. Ansell, a shadowy figure who never actually appears in *The Longest Journey,* and of Mr. Emerson, who is not entirely convincing because he is motherly rather than fatherly in his love for George, there are no effective fathers in the novels—for Gino's fatherhood is mythological and soon ends, and Mr. Wilcox's relation to Charles (in *Howards End*) is good but formal; on the other hand, Caroline Abbott's father is a nag, Rickie's father is cruel, and all the other fathers, to a remarkable number, are dead.

Of course it is possible that an American cannot judge fairly what a revolt against the English tradition of authority should be. The English father is said to be more dominant in the home than the American father; in England the school authority is stronger than here and expressed in corporal punishment; the firmness of English class lines is also significant; and perhaps most important of all is the necessity in a colonial empire of putting a premium on the authoritative type, even in its excess. Yet even taking into account these provocations to rebelliousness, we cannot but feel that through all of Forster's early novels we are being led away from officialism and stuffed-shirtism not toward maturity but toward youth. In none of his novels does Forster give us a mature hero. When George Emerson says that "youth matters intellectually" we want to reply that what matters intellectually is not youth and not age but rightness: we begin to feel that a certain irresponsibility is here at work.

Yet it is never entirely fair to invalidate a negative criticism by saying that it is not sufficiently positive—Forster's criticism of modern life is certainly not the less valid because he fails to exemplify what he means by the good life. What my comments do suggest, however, is that Forster, in the three early novels, has not fully done his job as a novelist: he represents the truth but he does not show the difficulties the truth must meet. And the criterion by which this judgment is made is a work of Forster's own: *Howards End* is a work of full responsibility. Its theme is "Only connect the prose and the passion," and it shows how almost hopelessly difficult it is to make this connection. That the insights of Forster's earlier novels could have come to face this difficulty is their justification.

Howards End is a novel about England's fate. It is a story of the class war. The war is latent but actual—so actual indeed that a sword is literally drawn and a man is really killed. England herself appears in the novel in palpable form, for the story moves by symbols and not only all its characters but also an elm, a marriage, a symphony, and a scholar's library stand for things beyond themselves. The symbol for England is the house whose name gives the title to the book. Like the plots of so many English novels, the plot of *Howards End* is about the rights of property, about a destroyed will-and-testament and rightful and wrongful heirs. It asks the question, "Who shall inherit England?"

The class struggle is not between the classes but within a single class, the middle class. Neither the aristocracy nor the proletariat is represented and the very poor are specifically barred—"We are not concerned with the very poor," the novelist says. "They are unthinkable, and only to be approached by the statistician or the poet. This story deals with gentlefolk, or with those who are obliged to pretend that they are gentlefolk." At the far end of the vast middle-class scale is Leonard Bast, the little clerk. He stands "at the extreme verge of gentility," at the very edge of the "abyss" of poverty. At the upper end of the scale is Mr. Wilcox, the business-man, rich and rapidly growing richer. Between are the Schlegels, Margaret and Helen, living comfortably on solid, adequate incomes. The Schlegels are intellectuals and constitute the point of consciousness of the novel; upon them the story balances, touching and connecting the wealthy middle class and the depressed middle class.

But the character who dominates the novel belongs to none of these groups. She is Mrs. Wilcox, who, despite her position in the story, soon leaves it. It is perhaps significant that her name is Ruth, for her heart is sad, the home for which she is sick is her chief passion and she stands amid alien corn. She herself is descended from the yeoman class to which Forster gives his strongest sympathies.

It is said of Ruth Wilcox by a "wise" character in the book, that she should have married a soldier, and Margaret Schlegel, who hated armies but liked soldiers, understands what is meant. For although Plato's *Republic* is not mentioned, it is nevertheless pervasive throughout the novel and Margaret, whose father had been a soldier before he became a philosopher, might well have remembered Plato's Watchdogs, the military Guardians from whom the philosophical Guardians were chosen; she might have remembered too that when the Just State is translated into the Just Man, the soldiers represent what Plato called the Spirited Element—the will, the love of honor and all generous things—which supports the reason.

Certainly the man Ruth Wilcox married had nothing of the Spirited Element in him. Henry Wilcox could give what his second wife in a moment of anger called an "unweeded kindness," but he lived the life of the Platonic Artisans, gainful, mediocre and unaware. The result for Ruth Wilcox was not frustration or unhappiness but tragedy, and her death was marked by cynicism, "not the superficial cynicism that snarls and sneers, but the cynicism that can go with courtesy and tenderness." Her husband had loved her, but his best praise had been for her "steadiness." Nor could her children draw on her for anything good. Her daughter Evie, handsome and tight-lipped, is a breeder of puppies, a dull and cruel girl; her younger son Paul, a vague figure in the novel, is a competent colonial administrator but a weak and foolish man; her elder son Charles is a bully and a righteous blunderer: her family, whom she loves and who adore her, are her alien corn. She is not sorry to die in her early fifties.

Mrs. Wilcox is not a clever woman—a whole scene is devoted to showing how clever people can even find her dull—and she is not, in the usual meaning of the word, a "sensitive" woman. But she has wisdom which is traditional and ancestral.

She seemed to belong not to the young people and their motor, but to the house and the trees that overshadowed it. One knew that she worshipped the past and that the instinctive wisdom the past alone can bestow had descended upon her—that wisdom to which we give the clumsy name of aristocracy. High born she might not be. But assuredly she cared about her ancestors and let them help her.

The house to which she "belongs" is a small though beautiful farm-house and her ancestors were simple people, yeomen, for Forster in this novel, as in *The Longest Journey*, puts his faith in the men of the English countryside.

Here men had been up since dawn. Their hours were ruled, not by a London office, but by the movements of the crops and sun. That they were men of the finest type only the sentimentalist can declare. But they kept to the life of daylight. They are England's hope. Clumsily they carry forward the torch of the sun, until such time as the nation sees fit to take it up. Half clodhopper, half boardschool prig, they can still throw back to a nobler stock, and breed yeomen.

As a character Ruth Wilcox is remarkably—and perhaps surprisingly—successful. Her "reality" is of a strange kind and consists in her having no reality in the ordinary sense—she does not have, that is, the reality of personality, of idiosyncrasy or even of power. Her strength comes exactly from her lack of force, her distinction from her lack of distinguishing traits. She suggests Shakespeare's "gentle" women, the Countess of *All's Well* or an older Imogen; or she has a touch of Chaucer's Griselda. It is appropriate that we find her kind in the past, for she represents England's past. But for all her lack of contemporary "reality," she is more successful as a real person than as a symbol; she must be seen to be believed and when she dies and becomes the brooding ghost of the story, she becomes a little trying, as perhaps all such symbolic spirits in novels do.

Before Mrs. Wilcox dies she has found the heir for her Howards End. She could not leave it to her family—"to them Howards End was a house: they could not know that to her it had been a spirit for which she sought a spiritual heir." As she lay on her death-bed she had penciled a note expressing the wish that the house go to Margaret Schlegel. To the Wilcox family nothing could have seemed a greater betrayal. For the Wilcoxes and the Schlegels had had dealings. They had met, joined for a moment when Paul and Helen had thought they were in love, and then had separated in a storm of "telegrams and anger." The Wilcoxes had been aware of how nearly they had been tricked in that affair. Now, with Ruth Wilcox's note before them, they must defend themselves again; they manage to convince themselves that the note should never have been written and is not binding; they destroy it and send Margaret Mrs. Wilcox's vinaigrette.

In the end Howards End comes to Margaret; but it is to pass beyond her to a little classless child, the son of Helen Schlegel and the pitiful Leonard Bast. For each of these intellectual sisters has reached out to the mysterious extremes of the middle class, Margaret upward to the Wilcoxes, Helen downward to the Basts. Such, in this novel, is their function as intellectuals.

Perhaps the intellectual first came into historical notice when Burke, attacking the French Revolution, spoke with contempt of the many small lawyers and small priests in the Assembly. They were, he said, merely men of mind, therefore ill-suited to the management of a state. Burke, we know, had a quarrel of long standing with the rational intellect and with those who used it. With his usual insight, he knew that a great change was coming about in the conduct of human affairs. The French Revolution was the first great occasion when Mind—conscious, verbalized mind—became an important element in national politics. Interest, of course, was also in play, and force too, but mind had the new function of generalizing interest and justifying force. And since Burke's day mind has played an increasing part in politics. Matthew Arnold spoke of the "idea-moved" masses of France and indeed ideas, far more than actual interests, have moved masses, so that even the most repressive and obscurantist systems are systems of ideas.

But the intellectual class does not descend only from the political priests and lawyers Burke attacked. Its origins are also to be found in the religious groups of the 18th century—further back than that, no doubt, in the beginnings of Protestantism: perhaps Erasmus and Milton are its true ancestors, but the 18th century witnessed such a notable breaking up of religious orthodoxies and such a transference of the religious feelings to secular life that it is surely the true seedtime of the intellectual as we now know him. One observes in the social circles of the first generation of English romantic poets the sense of morality, the large feelings and the intellectual energy that had once been given to religion.

This moral and pious aspect of the intellectual's tradition is important. Intellectuals as a class do not live by ideas alone but also by ideals. That is, they must desire the good not only for themselves but for all, and we might say that one of the truly new things in human life in the last two centuries is the politics of conscious altruism. To be sure, the sword and the stiletto have always had to be supplemented by this language, but the 18th century produced and the 19th century multiplied a class of people who sincerely thought or sincerely spoke of politics in terms of the freedom and privilege of groups less advantageously placed than their own; the word "underprivileged" is a key to the nature of the intellectual's political attitude.

Consequently, liberal intellectuals have always moved in an aura of self-congratulation. They sustain themselves by flattering themselves with intentions and they dismiss as "reactionary" whoever questions them. When the liberal intellectual thinks of himself, he thinks chiefly of his own good will and prefers not to know that the good will generates its own problems, that the love of humanity has its own vices and the love of truth its own insensibilities. The choice of the moral course does not settle the quality of morality; there is, as it were, a morality of morality.

And one of the complications of the intellectual's life is his relation to people who are not intellectuals. The very fact of being articulate, of making articulateness a preoccupation, sets up a barrier between the intellectual and the non-intellectual. The intellectual, the "freest" of men, consciously the most liberated from class, is actually the most class-marked and class-bound of all men. With the business-man his relation is likely to be unreal; the man who makes money can easily be worried by the intellectual's judgment of him, so pervasive and so coercive (up to a point) is the modern respect for the ideal of disinterestedness. And if we plumb the true feeling of the intellectual (it is not done often enough) we must see his own obscure admiration for the powers of the business-man. Then too, because the intellectual, whatever his social origin, always becomes a member of the middle class, he is obscurely aware how dependent is his existence upon the business civilization he is likely to fear and despise.

The relation of the intellectual to the lower classes is no less confused. There is a whole mass of mankind, the enormous majority, indeed, whom he considers it his duty to "protect." To these people he vaguely supposes himself to be in a benevolent superior relation, paternal, pedagogic, even priestlike. He believes it necessary to suppose that they are entirely good; the essential goodness of the masses is for him as much a certainty as the essential badness of the business classes. He is supposed to have nothing but the most benevolent feelings toward them; in *The Longest Journey,* for example, everyone is shocked when Stephen, who is a democrat but not an intellectual, feels the normal angry, aggressive emotions toward humble people. And so the intellectual, in addition to the barrier of his articulateness which cuts him off from the masses as well as from the middle classes, stands behind another barrier, the necessity of regarding the mass of men as objects of his benevolence.

The situation is sad but comic. It is the situation of the Schlegel sisters in *Howards End.* The comedy begins when Helen Schlegel is momentarily seduced by the Wilcox way of life. Visiting at Howards End, she finds her new friends strong; she likes them because they are all "keen on games" and because they put everything to use. Her own life of ideas seems suddenly inadequate.

She had liked giving in to Mr. Wilcox, or Evie or Charles; she had liked being told that her notions of life were sheltered or academic; that Equality was nonsense, Art and Literature nonsense. One by one the Schlegel fetiches had been overthrown, and, though professing to defend them, she rejoiced. When Mr. Wilcox said that one sound man of business did more good to the world than a dozen of your social reformers, she had swallowed the curious assertion without a gasp, and had leant back luxuriously among the cushions of his motor-car. When Charles said, "Why be polite to servants? they don't understand it," she had not given the Schlegel retort of, "If they don't understand it, I do." No; she vowed to be less polite to servants in the future. "I am swathed in cant," she thought, "and it is good for me to be stripped of it."

Actually, however, it was not a set of ideas that Helen was admiring—it was sex. It was with masculinity that she had fallen in love. It was the idea of men "taking hold," being efficient, having families and supporting them. Perhaps, too, of men owning motor-cars, for in 1910 the automobile is already the totem of the Wilcox males; it pervades the novel, but never attractively, and the Wilcox's chauffeur, Crane, in contrast to Shaw's genial Ennery Striker, is represented as a vaguely malevolent figure. Mr. Wilcox's smoking room, decorated to the masculine taste, is furnished with chairs of maroon leather, "as if a motor-car had spawned."

Howards End is not only a novel of the class war but of the war between men and women. Margaret, like Helen, is to respond to the Wilcox masculinity. Indeed, she marries Henry Wilcox. More perceptive than Helen, she knows this masculinity for what it is—far from adequate—but she accepts it more simply, demanding less of it. Perhaps neither of these young women would have been so urgent toward masculinity had their father lived or had their younger brother Tibby been brought up by a man to be manly. But they feared their own feminine lives and the clever men of their acquaintance offered them no escape. And so Helen, when she is kissed by Paul Wilcox in the garden of Howards End, is quite carried away. The normal life seems suddenly open to her, the life, one guesses, of the body.

It is so easy for an Englishman to sneer at these chance collisions of human beings. To the insular cynic and the insular moralist they offer an equal opportunity. It is so easy to talk about "passing emotion" and to forget how vivid the emotion was as it passed. Our impulse to sneer, to forget, is at root a good one. We recognize that emotion is not enough, and that men and women are personalities capable of sustained relations, not mere opportunities for an electrical discharge. Yet we rate the impulse too highly. We do not admit that by collisions of this trivial sort the doors of heaven may be shaken open. To Helen, at all events, her life was to bring nothing more intense than the embrace of this boy who played no part in it. . . . In time his slender personality faded, the scene that he evoked endured. In all the variable years that followed she never saw the like of it again.

Helen responded to the masculine principle, but it turned out not to be masculine at all. At breakfast next morning, Paul, who had a career to make in Africa, was frightened and abashed. To Helen the sight is never to be forgotten. "When that kind of man looks frightened, it is too awful. It is all right for us to be frightened, or for men of another sort—father, for instance; but for men like that!" She never does forget, though she thinks she does; the sexual betrayal by the Wilcoxes generates in her a hatred for Wilcoxism that is to make her act desperately, even insanely.

The sexual theme plays through the book, lightly, without much pressure save at one point, but with great seriousness. The great fact about the Wilcoxes is that which D. H. Lawrence saw, the fact of sexual deficiency. Paul with his fear, Charles with his silly wife, Dolly—"She was a rubbishy little creature, and she knew it"—Evie with her heavy love-banter, Mr. Wilcox with his lofty morality and his single, sordid, clandestine love-affair, all exhibit the deficiency.

The sexual lack has its concomitance and perhaps its result in the lack of a developed sense of personality. Helen says,

Perhaps the little thing that says "I" is missing out of the middle of their heads, and then it's a waste of time to blame them. There's a nightmare of a theory that says a special race is being born which will rule the rest of us in the future just because it lacks the little thing that says "I." There are two kinds of people—our kind, who live straight from the middle of their heads, and the other kind who can't because their heads have no middle. They can't say "I." They *aren't* in fact. . . . Pierpont Morgan has never said "I" in his life. No superman can say "I want" because "I want" must lead to the question "Who am I?" and so to Pity and to Justice. He only says "want"—"Want Europe," if he's Napoleon; "want wives" if he's Bluebeard; "want Botticelli" if he's Pierpont Morgan. Never "I" and if you could pierce through him, you'd find panic and emptiness in the middle.

She has no doubt been reading H. G. Wells with aversion and perhaps she has been having a bout with the romantic philosophers in her German father's library: certainly she makes an admirably accurate defense of the best of romantic egoism.

The recipient of her little speech is Leonard Bast on the night of the lowest ebb in his sad fortunes. Leonard is an insurance clerk whom the Schlegels had picked up in a concert-hall in a little farce of mistaken umbrellas and forgotten purses. The Schlegels had met the Wilcoxes touring a cathedral; they meet Leonard Bast at a concert: culture comically brings the middle class together and separates it. For Leonard is under the terrible necessity of being cultured.

This is the new obligation that democracy has brought. It will always be one of the mysteries of our civilization. Culture does not help us make our way in a business civilization, yet it has its value and yields its return. In our attitude toward the poet and the professor we are perfectly ambivalent: we know they are useless, yet they make us humble-defiant, and the business-man who declares himself a lowbrow is aggrieved if anyone agrees with him.

Leonard is "one of the thousands who have lost the life of the body and failed to reach the life of the spirit, who had given up the glory of the animal for a tail coat and a couple of ideas." His grandparents had been agricultural laborers, a fact of which he is ashamed; reading Ruskin is for him what a revival meeting was for his grandparents—he hopes for a sudden conversion, for the secret of life. When he touches the Schlegel world where art is breathed with the air and where ideas are not the secret of life but its very stuff, he is wholly confused. Margaret, as she observes him, questions all the 19th century's faith in education:

Culture had worked in her own case, but during the last few weeks she doubted whether it humanized the majority, so wide and widening is the gulf that stretches between the natural and the philosophic man, so many the good chaps who are wrecked trying to cross it. She knew the type very well—the aspirations, the mental dishonesty, the familiarity with the outsides of books.

What the Schlegel sisters cherished in Leonard was the solid grain of honesty under the pitiful overlay of culture. He has walked all one night to see the dawn in the country, moved by an impulse which was half native sensibility, half literary sentimentality. "'But was the dawn wonderful?'" Helen asks him. "With unforgettable sincerity he replied, 'No.' The word . . . flew like a pebble from the sling. Down toppled all that seemed ignoble or literary in his talk, down toppled tiresome R.L.S. and the 'love of the earth' and his silk top-hat." But Leonard cannot understand this of himself; indeed, he is not interested in himself, only in his soul. Just so he cannot be interested in the Schlegel girls except as sounding boards for his culture; in this he is like the Wilcoxes, for, like them, he is not aware of people but only of their status and function: he is obsessed by class. And even the Schlegel girls cannot see Leonard for his class; their very passion for democracy makes them less aware of him than of the abyss that is at his feet, the abyss of wasted lives, of "panic and emptiness" of which Helen especially is so conscious. Listening to the Allegro of Beethoven's Fifth Symphony, she hears its terror truthfully stated:

. . . The music started with a goblin walking quietly over the universe from end to end. Others followed him. They were not aggressive creatures; it was that that made them so horrible to Helen. They merely observed in passing that there was no such thing as splendour or heroism in the world. After the interlude of elephants dancing, they returned and made the observation for the second time. Helen could not contradict them, for, once at all events, she had felt the same, and had seen the reliable walls of youth collapse. Panic and emptiness! Panic and emptiness! The goblins were right.

Her brother raised his finger: it was the transitional passage on the drum.

For, as if things were going too far, Beethoven took hold of the goblins and made them do what he wanted. He appeared in person. He gave them a little push, and they began to walk in major key instead of in a minor, and then—he blew with his mouth and they were scattered! Gusts of splendour, gods and demi-gods contending with vast swords, colour and fragrance broadcast on the field of battle, magnificent victory, magnificent death! Oh, it all burst before the girl, and she even stretched out her gloved hands as if it were tangible. Any fate was titanic; and contest desirable; conqueror and conquered would alike be applauded by the angels of the utmost stars.

And the goblins—they had not really been there at all? They were only the phantoms of cowardice and unbelief? One healthy impulse would dispel them? Men like the Wilcoxes, or President Roosevelt would say yes. Beethoven knew better. The goblins had really been there. They might return—and they did. It was as if the splendour of life might boil over and waste to steam and froth. In its dissolution one heard the terrible, ominous note, and a goblin with increased malignity, walked quietly over the universe from end to end. Panic and emptiness! Panic and emptiness! Even the flaming ramparts of the world might fall.

Beethoven chose to make all right in the end. He built the ramparts up. He blew with his mouth for the second time, and again the goblins were scattered. . . . But the goblins were there. They could return. He had said so bravely, and that is why one can trust Beethoven when he says other things.[2]

Panic and emptiness make the dreadful fate that awaits people in this novel; they are the modern doom. And they threaten the unformed Leonard Bast as well as the cultivated Helen Schlegel.

Leonard is destroyed. The immediate cause of his destruction is Mr. Wilcox, who casually remarks to the sisters that Leonard's firm is unsound and advises that Leonard leave before the crash. The company turns out to be perfectly sound but Leonard has taken and lost another job and he and his wife Jacky fall quite destitute. Thus Helen finds them. Paul's betrayal has done its work on her; she hates all Wilcoxes, the idea of Margaret marrying Henry is inconceivable and when she fantastically drags the Basts to Henry's country place in Wales on the night of his daughter's wedding, her action is not so much humane as vengeful. Here the story takes its operatic turn, for poor Jacky is discovered to be Henry's former mistress and Margaret supports Henry in his refusal to help the Basts. That night Helen gives herself to Leonard, joylessly, out of an hysterical sense of justice.

Margaret's impulse toward Henry Wilcox is precisely the same as Helen's had been toward Paul, except that hers is more explicit and less sexually romantic. Henry is one of the race that runs the world,

[2] This would seem an apt occasion to mention Forster's belief that "music is the deepest of the arts and deep beneath the arts." Forster is himself a devoted amateur of the piano.

and he is masculine. She cannot continue to despise the people who control the ships and trains that carry "us literary people around." "More and more," she says, "do I refuse to draw my income and sneer at those who guarantee it." To be sure, it disturbs her that the man she is to marry thinks that both money and sex are unclean. He cannot talk directly about the one or feel at ease with the other. Yet she loves Henry and she looks for fulfillment in her marriage with him; she looks for reality. Writing to Helen at the time of the affair with Paul, she had said:

The truth is that there is a great outer life that you and I have never touched—a life in which telegrams and anger count. Personal relations, that we think are supreme, are not supreme there. There love means marriage settlements, death, death duties. So far I'm clear. But here my difficulty. This outer life, though obviously horrid, often seems the real one—there's grit in it. It does breed character. Do personal relationships lead to sloppiness in the end?

The outer life betrays Margaret; it is the inner life which "pays" and which, in the end, takes over the outer life. Howards End has for some time stood empty, a mere storage place for the Schlegels' furniture and their father's library. Miss Avery, the sibylline character who cares for the house, cherishing the memory of Ruth Wilcox and identifying Margaret with her, has arranged the furniture in the rooms and put the books on the shelves: thus, by the agency of women, the best of traditional England is furnished with the stuff of the intellect. And over the bookcase Miss Avery has hung the father's sword:[3] it was she who had said that Ruth Wilcox should have married a soldier. And in Howards End, thus furnished, Margaret and Helen meet after their long separation. For Helen has kept herself hidden from her family and has declared that she is going to live in Germany; Margaret, unable to understand the estrangement, has tempted her to Howards End to choose some souvenir of their old life before her departure. At the meeting she discovers that Helen is pregnant with Leonard's child. The recon-

[3] One cannot help thinking of Schiller's sword which Thackeray bought in Weimar and which he hung in his study over his books.

ciliation of the sisters precipitates what seems the end of Margaret's relation with Henry, for Helen wishes to spend the night among their old possessions and, although Henry has no feeling except ownership for Howards End, he refuses to have it desecrated by Helen's presence.

The outer life that fails Margaret now fails itself; but the inner life comes to its rescue. Leonard, torn by remorse over his relation with Helen, comes down to Howards End to confess to Margaret. The dull moral blunderer, Charles Wilcox, is in the library when Bast arrives. Knowing Leonard to be Helen's "lover," he snatches down the old Schlegel sabre to beat him with the flat. Leonard dies, not of the blow but of a weak heart, and as he drops he clutches the bookcase which falls and sends the books tumbling down on him in a shower—the books that in life had promised him so much and given him so little. Charles is jailed for manslaughter and his father, quite broken, relies wholly on Margaret, who establishes him in Howards End together with Helen and Helen's baby.

Not for nothing do Margaret and Helen bear the names of the heroines of the two parts of *Faust,* one the heroine of the practical life, the other of the ideal life; Henry Wilcox bears Faust's Christian name and he and Leonard together, the practical man and the seeker after experience, make up the composite hero. Helen's child is the Euphorion—he is the heir not only of Leonard Bast but of Henry Wilcox, for Howards End is to go to Margaret and from her to Helen's child. And the Eternal Feminine has taken complete control of the England which the masculine outer life has so sadly muddled. It is not entirely a happy picture on which Forster concludes, this rather contrived scene of busyness and contentment in the hayfield; the male is too thoroughly gelded and, of the two women, Helen confesses that she cannot love a man, Margaret that she cannot love a child. And the rust of London, with its grim promise of modern life "melted down, all over the world," creeps toward Howards End. Meanwhile the Euphorion, the classless heir of all the classes in this novel, plays in the hayfield and suggests a hope. He is not only the symbol of the classless society but, as he takes his pleasure among the busy workers in the hay, he is also the symbol of the "Only connect!" which was Margaret's clue to the good life. "Only connect the prose and the passion, and both will be exalted, and human love will be seen at its height."

CHAPTER EIGHT

A Passage to India

THE YEARS between 1910 and 1914 were the vestibule to what Forster has called "the sinister corridor of our age." *Howards End* records the sense of Germany's growing strength; Mr. Schlegel, father of Helen and Margaret, had voluntarily exiled himself from the old Germany of philosophers, musicians and little courts and he spoke bitterly of the new imperialism to which "money [was] supremely useful; intellect, rather useful; imagination, of no use at all."

Not many books of the time were so precisely sensitive to the situation, yet a kind of sultry premonitory hush comes over literature in these years. The hope of the first decade of the century has been checked. The athletic quality of intelligence which seemed to mark the work of even five years earlier has subsided.

In 1910, following the publication of *Howards End,* Forster projected two novels but wrote neither. The next year he finished a play, *The Heart of Bosnia,* which, by his own account, was not good, although it almost reached the stage in 1914; plans for its production were abandoned at the outbreak of war and the manuscript was lost by the producer. In 1912, Forster, in company with Dickinson and R. C. Trevelyan, sailed for India. Dickinson, traveling on one of the fellowships established by Albert Kahn in the interests of international understanding, had official visits and tours to make and the friends separated at Bombay. But their itineraries crossed several times and they spent a fortnight as guests of the Maharajah of Chhatarpur, who loved Dickinson and philosophy—"Tell me, Mr. Dickinson, where is God?" the Maharajah said. "Can Herbert Spencer lead me to him, or should I prefer George Henry Lewes? Oh when will Krishna come and be my friend? Oh Mr. Dickinson!"

The two travelers came away from India with widely different feelings. Dickinson, who was to love China, was not comfortable in India. Displeased as he was by her British rulers, he was not pleased with India itself. "There is no solution to the problem of governing India," he wrote. "Our presence is a curse both to them and to us. Our going away will be worse. I believe that to the last word. And *why* can't the races meet? Simply because the Indians *bore* the English. That is the simple adamantine fact." It is not an enlightening or even a serious view of the situation, and Forster, dissenting from it, speaks of the "peace and happiness" which he himself found in India in 1912 and again on his second visit ten years later.

The best fruit of the Indian journey was to be *A Passage to India,* but meanwhile Forster wrote several short pieces on Indian life of which two, "The Suppliant" and "Advance, India!" (both reprinted in *Abinger Harvest*), admirably depict the comic, sad confusion of a nation torn between two cultures.

He began to sketch the Indian novel, but the war postponed its completion for a decade. And the war quite destroyed the project for a critical study of Samuel Butler, with whose mind Forster's has community at so many points. But the war, which sent Forster to non-combatant service in Egypt, developed in him the interest in Imperial conduct and policy which the Indian tour had begun. Hitherto Forster's political concern had been intense but perhaps abstract; now it became increasingly immediate. The three Egyptian years gave him not only the material for two books and many essays, but also a firm position on the Imperial question.

The first of Forster's Egyptian books is the guidebook, *Alexandria;*

its introductory account of the city's history gives Forster the opportunity to display his love of the Hellenic and naturalistic, his contempt for the Christian and theological; its second part arranges tours to points of interest, and the whole job is scholarly, attractive and efficient.[1] Much less can be said for *Pharos and Pharillon,* another venture into Alexandrian history and local color. The volume is infused with the archness which has been noted earlier as the fault of Forster's first historical essays; the years have but intensified it. Under Forster's implacable gentleness, the past becomes what it should never be, quaint, harmless and ridiculous. Menelaos, Alexander, the Ptolemies, the Jews, the Arabs, the Christian theologians, the very lighthouse itself all become submerged in high irony. This desperately persistent fault of taste is all the more surprising because Forster has himself so rightly characterized it in one of his best essays, "The Consolations of History."

It is pleasant to be transferred from an office where one is afraid of a sergeant-major into an office where one can intimidate generals, and perhaps that is why History is so attractive to the more timid among us. We can recover self-confidence by snubbing the dead. . . . Tight little faces from Oxford, fish-shaped faces from Cambridge,—we cannot help having our dreams.

The same fault of lofty whimsicality inheres in other of the sketches which in *Arbinger Harvest* are collected under the rubric of "The Past." Sufficiently objectionable in "Captain Edward Gibbon" and in "Voltaire's Laboratory," it becomes really bad in "Trooper Silas Tompkyns Comberbacke" and in "The Abbeys' Difficulties," the first of which dramatically reveals the open secret that the Trooper's real name was Samuel Taylor Coleridge, the second that the young people with whom the Abbeys had difficulty were Fanny and John Keats.

---

[1] The historical part of the book is a model of popularization without condescension. Especially notable are the lucid pages on the Alexandrian mystics; the exposition of Plotinus has the quality of creative insight into mystical thought that makes *A Passage to India* so remarkable. It is worth noting that Dickinson in his youth was an enthusiastic student of Plotinus.

A single sentence of *Pharos and Pharillon* points away from this slim, feasting antiquarianism; speaking of Fort Kait Bey, Forster mentions the holes in it "made by Admiral Seymour when he bombarded the Fort in 1882 and laid the basis of our intercourse with modern Egypt." In 1920 Forster wrote his note for *The Government of Egypt,* a pamphlet of the International Section of the Labour Research Department, a Fabian organization. Although it does little save support the Committee's recommendation that Egypt be given either dominion status or autonomy and although it is scarcely interesting in itself, it indicates Forster's increasing interest in public affairs.

It was an angry interest. In 1934 Forster was to publish his biography of Dickinson, who had died two years before. Perhaps because Dickinson's life lacked tension or tone, perhaps because Forster wrote under some reserve, the biography is not a work of high distinction, but it serves to suggest the political atmosphere in which Forster lived. The crown of Dickinson's political life was his fight against what he called International Anarchy; his weapon, soon taken from his hands, was the League of Nations. He hoped to raise the minds of men above "the fighting attitude" of practical politics, but he could never, he confessed, formulate clearly "the great problem of the relation of ideals to passion and interest." This is, of course, Forster's own insistent question, but Forster's is an angrier mind than Dickinson's and any uncertainty he feels about the ultimate problems of politics does not prevent him from speaking out on matters of the moment.

England after the war was tense with class antagonism. In 1920 Forster became for a year the literary editor of the *Daily Herald,* a Labor paper to whose weekly literary page many well-known writers of liberal leanings contributed reviews. In the following years the amount of Forster's literary and political journalism, collected and uncollected, was considerable.

The political pieces are suffused with disillusionment about the war, a foreboding that a new war is imminent, a hatred of the stu-

pidities of class rule. They pretend neither to originality of sentiment nor to practical perspicacity; they express, sometimes with
anger, sometimes with bitterness, sometimes only with a kind of
salutary irritation and disgust, the old emotions—the 19th-century
emotions, we almost feel, and we salute their directness—of a rational democrat confronting foolishness and pretense. Perhaps the
most successful of these pieces is the essay "Me, Them and You." It
is a review of the Sargent exhibition of 1925 in which, among all
the aristocratic portraits, Sargent's pleasant, fanciful war picture,
"Gassed," was hung. The situation was made for the satirist and
Forster takes advantage of it in one of the truly successful pieces of
modern invective.

The portraits dominated. Gazing at each other over our heads, they
said, "What would the country do without us? We have got the decora-
tions and the pearls, we make fashions and wars, we have the largest
houses and eat the best food, and control the most important industries,
and breed the most valuable children, and ours is the Kingdom and the
Power and the Glory." And, listening to their chorus, I felt this was so,
and my clothes fitted worse and worse, and there seemed in all the universe no gulf wider than the gulf between Them and Me—no wider
gulf, until I encountered You.

You had been plentiful enough in the snow outside (your proper place)
but I had not expected to find You here in the place of honour, too. Yours
was by far the largest picture in the show. You were hung between Lady
Cowdray and the Hon. Mrs. Langman, and You were entitled "Gassed."
You were of godlike beauty—for the upper classes only allow the lower
classes to appear in art on condition that they wash themselves and have
classical features. These conditions you fulfilled. A line of golden-haired
Apollos moved along a duck-board from left to right with bandages over
their eyes. They had been blinded by mustard gas. Others sat peacefully
in the foreground, others approached through the middle distance. The
battlefield was sad but tidy. No one complained, no one looked lousy or
overtired, and the aeroplanes overhead struck the necessary note of the
majesty of England. It was all that a great war picture should be, and it
was modern because it managed to tell a new sort of lie. Many ladies and
gentlemen fear that Romance is passing out of war with the sabres and
the chargers. Sargent's masterpiece reassures them. He shows them that
it is possible to suffer with a quiet grace under the new conditions, and

Lady Cowdray and the Hon. Mrs. Langman, as they looked over the twenty feet of canvas that divided them, were able to say, "How touching," instead of "How obscene."

Less remarkable but filled with a fine irritation is the piece on the British Empire Exhibition at Wembley ("An Empire Is Born") and another on the Queen's Doll House ("The Doll Souse"). Forster's old antipathy to the clergy turns up again in political form in the verses which answer Bishop Welldon's public complaint of the profanity of the Labor members of Parliament. One of the best of his essays, "My Wood," describes the growth of the property sense in himself after the purchase of a new tract of wood—"The other day I heard a twig snap in [my wood]. I was annoyed at first, for I thought that someone was blackberrying, and depreciating the value of the undergrowth. On coming nearer, I saw it was not a man who had trodden on the twig and snapped it, but a bird, and I felt pleased. My bird." The essay is especially to be noted because it states with almost startling explicitness a view of life which has been implicit in the novels:

> Our life on earth is, and ought to be, material and carnal. But we have not yet learned to manage our materialism and carnality properly; they are still entangled with the desire for ownership; where (in the words of Dante) "Possession is one with loss."

Over the anomalies of literary censorship Forster had long been exercised.[2] In 1939 he was appointed by the Lord Chancellor to the Committee to examine the Law of Defamatory Libel. His 1935 address to the Paris *Congrès International des Écrivains* on the subject of literary freedom constitutes a declaration of political faith.

> It seems to me that if nations keep on amassing armaments, they can no more help discharging their filth than an animal which keeps on eating can stop itself from excreting. This being so, my job and the job of those who feel with me is an interim job. We have just to go on tinkering as well as we can with our old tools until the crash comes. When the crash comes, nothing is any good. After it—if there is an after—the task

---

[2] He deals with censorship in "Mrs. Grundy at the Parkers'" (*Abinger Harvest*) and in his introduction to Alec Craig's *The Banned Books of England* (1937).

of civilization will be carried on by people whose training has been different from my own.

I am worried by thoughts of a war oftener than by thoughts of my own death, yet the line to be adopted over both these nuisances is the same. One must behave as if one is immortal, and as if civilization is eternal. Both statements are false—I shall not survive, no more will the great globe itself—both of them must be assumed to be true if we are to go on eating and working and travelling, and keep open a few breathing holes for the human spirit.

In 1922 Forster made a second journey to India and took up again the Indian story he had projected. *A Passage to India* appeared with great success in 1924.

A Passage to India is Forster's best known and most widely read novel. Public and political reasons no doubt account for this; in England the book was a matter for controversy and its success in America, as Forster himself explains it, was due to the superiority Americans could feel at the English botch of India. But the public, political nature of the book is not extraneous; it inheres in the novel's very shape and texture.

By many standards of criticism, this public, political quality works for good. *A Passage to India* is the most comfortable and even the most conventional of Forster's novels. It is under the control not only of the author's insight; a huge, hulking physical fact which he is not alone in seeing, requires that the author submit to its veto-power. Consequently, this is the least surprising of Forster's novels, the least capricious and, indeed, the least personal. It quickly establishes the pattern for our emotions and keeps to it. We are at once taught to withhold our sympathies from the English officials, to give them to Mrs. Moore and to the "renegade" Fielding, to regard Adela Quested with remote interest and Aziz and his Indian friends with affectionate understanding.

Within this pattern we have, to be sure, all the quick, subtle modifications, the sudden strictnesses or relentings of judgment which are the best stuff of Forster's social imagination. But always the pattern remains public, simple and entirely easy to grasp. What distinguishes it from the patterns of similarly public and political novels is the rigor of its objectivity; it deals with unjust, hysterical emotion and it leads us, not to intense emotions about justice, but to cool poise and judgment—if we do not relent in our contempt for Ronny, we are at least forced to be aware that he is capable of noble, if stupid, feelings; the English girl who has the hallucination of an attempted rape by a native has engaged our sympathy by her rather dull decency; we are permitted no easy response to the benign Mrs. Moore, or to Fielding, who stands out against his own people, or to the native physician who is wrongly accused. This restraint of our emotions is an important element in the book's greatness.

With the public nature of the story goes a chastened and somewhat more public style than is usual with Forster, and a less arbitrary manner. Forster does not abandon his right to intrude into the novel, but his manner of intrusion is more circumspect than ever before. Perhaps this is because here, far less than in the English and Italian stories, he is in possession of truth; the Indian gods are not his gods, they are not genial and comprehensible. So far as the old Mediterranean deities of wise impulse and loving intelligence can go in India, Forster is at home; he thinks they can go far but not all the way, and a certain retraction of the intimacy of his style reflects his uncertainty. The acts of imagination by which Forster conveys the sense of the Indian gods are truly wonderful; they are, nevertheless, the acts of imagination not of a master of the truth but of an intelligent neophyte, still baffled.

So the public nature of the novel cannot be said to work wholly for good. For the first time Forster has put himself to the test of verisimilitude. Is this the truth about India? Is this the way the English act?—always? sometimes? never? Are Indians like this?—all of them? some of them? Why so many Moslems and so few Hindus? Why so much Hindu religion and so little Moslem? And then, finally, the disintegrating question, What is to be done?

Forster's gallery of English officials has of course been disputed in England; there have been many to say that the English are not like that. Even without knowledge we must suppose that the Indian Civil Service has its quota of decent, devoted and humble officials.

But if Forster's portraits are perhaps angry exaggerations, anger can be illuminating—the English of Forster's Chandrapore are the limits toward which the English in India must approach, for Lord Acton was right, power does corrupt, absolute power does corrupt absolutely.

As for the representation of the Indians, that too can be judged here only on *a priori* grounds. Although the Indians are conceived in sympathy and affection, they are conceived with these emotions alone, and although all of them have charm, none of them has dignity; they touch our hearts but they never impress us. Once, at his vindication feast, Aziz is represented as "full of civilization . . . complete, dignified, rather hard" and for the first time Fielding treats him "with diffidence," but this only serves to remind us how lacking in dignity Aziz usually is. Very possibly this is the effect that Indians make upon even sensitive Westerners; Dickinson, as we have seen, was bored by them, and generations of subjection can diminish the habit of dignity and teach grown men the strategy of the little child.

These are not matters that we can settle; that they should have arisen at all is no doubt a fault of the novel. Quite apart from the fact that questions of verisimilitude diminish illusion, they indicate a certain inadequacy in the conception of the story. To represent the official English as so unremittingly bad and the Indians as so unremittingly feeble is to prevent the story from being sufficiently worked out in terms of the characters; the characters, that is, are *in* the events, the events are not in them: we want a larger Englishman than Fielding, a weightier Indian than Aziz.

These are faults, it is true, and Forster is the one novelist who could commit them and yet transcend and even put them to use. The relation of the characters to the events, for example, is the result of a severe imbalance in the relation of plot to story. Plot and story in this novel are not coextensive as they are in all Forster's other novels.[3] The plot is precise, hard, crystallized and far simpler

[3] I am not using plot and story in exactly the same sense that Forster uses them in *Aspects of the Novel*.

Story is beneath the plot

than any Forster has previously conceived. The story is beneath and above the plot and continues beyond it in time. It is, to be sure, created by the plot, it is the plot's manifold reverberation, but it is greater than the plot and contains it. The plot is as decisive as a judicial opinion; the story is an impulse, a tendency, a perception. The suspension of plot in the large circumambient sphere of story, the expansion of the story from the center of plot, requires some of the subtlest manipulation that any novel has ever had. This relation of plot and story tells us that we are dealing with a political novel of an unusual kind. The characters are of sufficient size for the plot; they are not large enough for the story—and that indeed is the point of the story.

This, in outline, is the plot: Adela Quested arrives in India under the chaperonage of the elderly Mrs. Moore with whose son by a first marriage Adela has an "understanding." Both ladies are humane and Adela is liberal and they have an intense desire to "know India." This is a matter of some annoyance to Ronny, Mrs. Moore's son and Adela's fiancé, and of amused condescension to the dull people at the station who try to satisfy the ladies with elephant rides—only very *new* people try to *know* India. Both Mrs. Moore and Adela are chilled by Ronny; he has entirely adopted the point of view of the ruling race and has become a heavy-minded young judge with his dull dignity as his chief recognized asset. But despite Ronny's fussy certainty about what is and is not proper, Mrs. Moore steps into a mosque one evening and there makes the acquaintance of Aziz, a young Moslem doctor. Aziz is hurt and miserable, for he has just been snubbed; Mrs. Moore's kindness and simplicity soothe him. Between the two a friendship develops which politely includes Adela Quested. At last, by knowing Indians, the travelers will know India, and Aziz is even more delighted than they at the prospect of the relationship. To express his feelings he organizes a fantastically elaborate jaunt to the Marabar Caves. Fielding, the principal of the local college, and Professor Godbole, a Hindu teacher, were also to have been of the party but they miss the train and Aziz goes ahead with the ladies and his absurd retinue. In one of the caves Mrs.

Moore has a disturbing psychic experience and sends Aziz and
Adela to continue the exploration without her. Adela, not a very
attractive girl, has had her doubts about her engagement to Ronny,
not a very attractive man, and now she ventures to speak of love to
Aziz, quite abstractly but in a way both to offend him and disturb
herself. In the cave the strap of her field-glasses is pulled and broken
by someone in the darkness and she rushes out in a frenzy of hallucination that Aziz has attempted to rape her. The accusation makes
the English of the station hysterical with noble rage. In every English mind there is the certainty that Aziz is guilty and the verdict
is foregone. Only Fielding and Mrs. Moore do not share this certainty. Fielding, because of his liking for the young doctor, and Mrs.
Moore, because of an intuition, are sure that the event could not
have happened and that Adela is the victim of illusion. Fielding,
who openly declares his partisanship, is ostracized, and Mrs. Moore,
who only hints her opinion, is sent out of the country by her son;
the journey in the terrible heat of the Indian May exhausts her and
she dies on shipboard. At the trial Adela's illusion, fostered by the
mass-hysteria of the English, becomes suddenly dispelled, she recants,
Aziz is cleared, Fielding is vindicated and promoted, the Indians
are happy, the English furious.

Thus the plot. And no doubt it is too much a plot of event, too
easily open and shut. Nevertheless it is an admirable if obvious
device for organizing an enormous amount of observation of both
English and native society; it brings to spectacular virulence the
latent antagonisms between rulers and ruled.

Of the Anglo-Indian society it is perhaps enough to say that,
"more than it can hope to do in England," it lives by the beliefs of
the English public school. It is arrogant, ignorant, insensitive—intelligent natives estimate that a year in India makes the pleasantest
Englishman rude. And of all the English it is the women who insist
most strongly on their superiority, who are the rawest and crudest
in their manner. The men have a certain rough liking for the men
of the subject race; for instance, Turton, Collector of the district,
has "a contemptuous affection for the pawns he had moved about

for so many years; they must be worth his pains." But the women, unchecked by any professional necessity or pride, think wholly in terms of the most elementary social prestige and Turton's wife lives for nothing else. "After all," Turton thinks but never dares say, "it's our women who make everything more difficult out here."

This is the result of the undeveloped heart. *A Passage to India* is not a radical novel; its data were gathered in 1912 and 1922, before the full spate of Indian nationalism; it is not concerned to show that the English should not be in India at all. Indeed, not until the end of the book is the question of the expulsion of the English mentioned, and the novel proceeds on an imperialistic premise—ironically, for it is not actually Forster's own—its chief point being that by reason of the undeveloped heart the English have thrown away the possibility of holding India. For want of a smile an Empire is to be lost.[4] Not even justice is enough. "Indians know whether they are liked or not," Fielding says, "—they cannot be fooled here. Justice never satisfies them, and that is why the British Empire rests on sand." Mrs. Moore listens to Ronny defending the British attitude; "His words without his voice might have impressed her, but when she heard the self-satisfied lilt of them, when she saw the mouth moving so complacently and competently beneath the little red nose, she felt, quite illogically, that this was not the last word on India. One touch of regret—not the canny substitute but the true regret—would have made him a different man, and the British Empire a different institution."

Justice is not enough then, but in the end neither are liking and good will enough. For although Fielding and Aziz reach out to each

[4] H. N. Brailsford in his *Rebel India* (1931) deals at some length with the brutality with which demonstrations were put down in 1930. "Here and there," he says, "mildness and good-temper disarmed the local agitation. I heard of one magistrate, very popular with the people, who successfully treated the defiance of the Salt Monopoly as a joke. The local Congress leaders made salt openly in front of his bungalow. He came out: bought some of the contraband salt: laughed at its bad quality: chaffed the bystanders, and went quietly back to his house. The crowd melted away, and no second attempt was made to defy this genial bureaucrat. On the other hand, any exceptional severity, especially if physical brutality accompanied it, usually raised the temper of the local movement and roused it to fresh daring and further sacrifices." (P. 7, footnote.)

other in friendship, a thousand little tricks of speech, a thousand different assumptions and different *tempi* keep them apart. They do not understand each other's *amounts* of emotion, let alone kinds of emotion. "Your emotions never seem in proportion to their objects, Aziz," Fielding says, and Aziz answers, "Is emotion a sack of potatoes, so much the pound, to be measured out?"

The theme of separateness, of fences and barriers, the old theme of the Pauline epistles, which runs through all Forster's novels, is, in *A Passage to India,* hugely expanded and everywhere dominant. The separation of race from race, sex from sex, culture from culture, even of man from himself, is what underlies every relationship. The separation of the English from the Indians is merely the most dramatic of the chasms in this novel. Hindu and Moslem cannot really approach each other; Aziz, speaking in all friendliness to Mr. Das, the Magistrate, wishes that Hindus did not remind him of cowdung, and the Hindu Mr. Das thinks, "'Some Moslems are very violent'"—"Between people of distant climes there is always the possibility of romance, but the various branches of Indians know too much about each other to surmount the unknowable easily." Adela and Ronny cannot meet in sexuality, and when, after the trial, Adela and Fielding meet in an idea, "a friendliness, as of dwarfs shaking hands, was in the air." Fielding, when he marries Mrs. Moore's daughter Stella, will soon find himself apart from his young wife. And Mrs. Moore is separated from her son, from all people, from God, from the universe.

This sense of separateness broods over the book, pervasive, symbolic—at the end the very earth requires, and the sky approves, the parting of Aziz and Fielding—and perhaps accounts for the remoteness of the characters: they are so far from each other that they cannot reach us. But the isolation is not merely adumbrated; in certain of its aspects it is very precisely analyzed and some of the most brilliant and virtuose parts of the novel are devoted to the delineation of Aziz and his friends, to the investigation of the cultural differences that keep Indian and Englishman apart.

The mould for Aziz is Gino Carella of the first novel. It is the mould of un-Englishness, that is to say, of volatility, tenderness, sensibility, a hint of cruelty, much warmth, a love of pathos, the desire to please even at the cost of insincerity. Like Gino's, Aziz's nature is in many ways child-like, in many ways mature: it is mature in its acceptance of child-like inconsistency. Although eager to measure up to English standards of puritan rectitude, Aziz lives closer to the literal facts of his emotions; for good or bad, he is more human. He, like his friends, is not prompt, not efficient, not neat, not really convinced of Western ideas even in science—when he retires to a native state he slips back to mix a little magic with his medicine—and he, like them, is aware of his faults. He is hyper-sensitive, imagining slights even when there are none because there have actually been so many; he is full of humility and full of contempt and desperately wants to be liked. He is not heroic but his heroes are the great chivalrous emperors, Babur and Alamgir. In short, Aziz is a member of a subject race. A rising nationalism in India may by now have thrust him aside in favor of a more militant type; but we can be sure that if the new type has repudiated Aziz's emotional contradictions it has not resolved them.

Aziz and his friends are Moslems, and with Moslems of the business and professional class the plot of the novel deals almost entirely. But the story is suffused with Hinduism.[5] It is Mrs. Moore who carries the Hindu theme; it is Mrs. Moore, indeed, who is the story. The theme is first introduced by Mrs. Moore observing a wasp.

Going to hang up her cloak she found that the tip of the peg was occupied by a small wasp. . . . There he clung, asleep, while jackals in the plain bayed their desires and mingled with the percussion of drums.

"Pretty dear," said Mrs. Moore to the wasp. He did not wake, but her voice floated out, to swell the night's uneasiness.

[5] The Indian masses appear only as crowds in the novel; they have no individualized representative except the silent, unthinking figure of the man who pulls the *punkah* in the courtroom scene. He is one of the "untouchables" though he has the figure of a god, and in Adela's mind, just before the crisis of the trial, he raises doubts of the "suburban Jehovah" who sanctifies her opinions, and he makes her think of Mrs. Moore.

This wasp is to recur in Professor Godbole's consciousness when he has left Chandrapore and taken service as director of education in a Hindu native state. He stands, his school quite forgotten—turned into a granary, indeed—and celebrates the birth of Krishna in the great religious festival that dominates the third part of the novel.[6] The wasp is mixed up in his mind—he does not know how it got there in the first place, nor do we—with a recollection of Mrs. Moore.

He was a Brahman, she a Christian, but it made no difference, it made no difference whether she was a trick of his memory or a telepathic appeal. It was his duty, as it was his desire, to place himself in the position of the God and to love her, and to place himself in her position and say to the God: "Come, come, come, come." This was all he could do. How inadequate! But each according to his own capacities, and he knew that his own were small. "One old Englishwoman and one little, little wasp," he thought, as he stepped out of the temple into the grey of a pouring wet morning. "It does not seem much, still it is more than I am myself."

The presence of the wasp, first in Mrs. Moore's consciousness, then in Godbole's, Mrs. Moore's acceptance of the wasp, Godbole's acceptance of Mrs. Moore—in some symbolic fashion, this is the thread of the story of the novel as distinguished from its plot. For the story is essentially concerned with Mrs. Moore's discovery that Christianity is not adequate. In a quiet way, Mrs. Moore is a religious woman; at any rate, as she has grown older she has found it "increasingly difficult to avoid" mentioning God's name "as the greatest she knew." Yet in India God's name becomes less and less efficacious—"Outside the arch there seemed always another arch, beyond the remotest echo a silence."

And so, unwittingly, Mrs. Moore has moved closer and closer to Indian ways of feeling. When Ronny and Adela go for an automobile ride with the Nawab Bahadur and the chauffeur swerves at something in the path and wrecks the car, Mrs. Moore, when she is told of the incident, remarks without thinking, "A ghost!" And a ghost it was, or so the Nawab believed, for he had run over and

[6] The novel is divided: I. Mosque, II. Caves, III. Temple. In his notes to the Everyman edition Forster points out that the three parts correspond to the three Indian seasons.

killed a drunken man at that spot nine years before. "None of the English knew of this, nor did the chauffeur; it was a racial secret communicable more by blood than by speech." This "racial secret" has somehow been acquired by Mrs. Moore. And the movement away from European feeling continues: "She felt increasingly (vision or nightmare?) that, though people are important, the relations between them are not, and that in particular too much fuss has been made over marriage; centuries of carnal embracement, yet man is no nearer to understanding man." The occasion of her visit to the Marabar Caves is merely the climax of change, although a sufficiently terrible one.

What so frightened Mrs. Moore in the cave was an echo. It is but one echo in a book which is contrived of echoes. Not merely does Adela Quested's delusion go in company with a disturbing echo in her head which only ceases when she masters her delusion, but the very texture of the story is a reticulation of echoes. Actions and speeches return, sometimes in a better, sometimes in a worse form, given back by the perplexing "arch" of the Indian universe. The recurrence of the wasp is a prime example, but there are many more. If Aziz plays a scratch game of polo with a subaltern who comes to think well of this particular anonymous native, the same subaltern will be particularly virulent in his denunciation of Aziz the rapist, never knowing that the liked and the detested native are the same. If the natives talk about their inability to catch trains, an Englishman's missing a train will make all the trouble of the story. Mrs. Moore will act with bad temper to Adela and with surly indifference to Aziz, but her action will somehow have a good echo; and her children will be her further echo. However we may interpret Forster's intention in this web of reverberation, it gives his book a cohesion and intricacy usually only found in music. And of all the many echoes, the dominant one is the echo that booms through the Marabar cave.

A Marabar cave had been horrid as far as Mrs. Moore was concerned, for she had nearly fainted in it, and had some difficulty in preventing herself from saying so as soon as she got into the air again. It was natural enough; she had always suffered from faintness, and the cave had become too full, because all their retinue followed them. Crammed with villagers and servants, the circular chamber began to smell. She lost Aziz and Adela in the dark, didn't know who touched her, couldn't breathe, and some vile naked thing struck her face and settled on her mouth like a pad. She tried to regain the entrance tunnel, but an influx of villagers swept her back. She hit her head. For an instant she went mad, hitting and gasping like a fanatic. For not only did the crush and stench alarm her; there was also a terrifying echo.

Professor Godbole had never mentioned an echo; it never impressed him, perhaps. There are some exquisite echoes in India; . . . The echo in a Marabar cave is not like these, it is entirely devoid of distinction. Whatever is said, the same monotonous noise replies, and quivers up and down the walls until it is absorbed in the roof. "Boum" is the sound as far as the human alphabet can express it, or "bou-oum," or "ou-boum"— utterly dull. Hope, politeness, the blowing of a nose, the squeal of a boot, all produce "boum."

Panic and emptiness—Mrs. Moore's panic had been at the emptiness of the universe. And one goes back beyond Helen Schlegel's experience of the Fifth Symphony in *Howards End:* the negating mess of the cave reminds us of and utterly denies the mess of that room in which Caroline Abbott saw Gino with his child. For then the mess had been the source of life and hope, and in it the little child had blossomed; Caroline had looked into it from the "charnel chamber" of the reception room and the "light in it was soft and large, as from some gracious, noble opening." It is, one might say, a representation of the womb and a promise of life. There is also a child in the mess of the Marabar cave—for the "vile, naked thing" that settles "like a pad" on Mrs. Moore's mouth is "a poor little baby, astride its mother's hip." The cave's opening is behind Mrs. Moore, she is facing into the grave; light from the world does not enter, and the universe of death makes all things alike, even life and death, even good and evil.

. . . The echo began in some indescribable way to undermine her hold on life. . . . It had managed to murmur: "Pathos, piety, courage—they exist, but are identical, and so is filth. Everything exists, nothing has value." If one had spoken vileness in that place, or quoted lofty poetry,

the comment would have been the same—"ou-boum." If one had spoken
with the tongues of angels and pleaded for all the unhappiness and mis-
understanding in the world, past, present, and to come; for all the misery
men must undergo whatever their opinion and position, and however
much they dodge or bluff—it would amount to the same. . . . Devils
are of the north, and poems can be written about them, but no one could
romanticize the Marabar because it robbed infinity and eternity of their
vastness, the only quality that accommodates them to mankind. . . . But
suddenly at the edge of her mind, religion reappeared, poor little talka-
tive Christianity, and she knew that all its divine words from "Let there
be Light" to "It is finished" only amounted to "boum."

"Something snub-nosed, incapable of generosity," had spoken to
her—"the undying worm itself." Converse with God, her children,
Aziz, is repugnant to her. She wants attention for her sorrow and
rejects it when given. Knowing Aziz to be innocent, she says nothing in his behalf except a few sour words that upset Adela's certainty, and though she knows that her testimony will be useful to
Aziz, she allows Ronny to send her away. She has had the beginning
of the Hindu vision of things and it has crushed her. What the
Hindu vision is, is expressed by Professor Godbole to Fielding:

> Good and evil are different, as their names imply. But, in my own
> humble opinion, they are both of them aspects of my Lord. He is present
> in the one, absent in the other, and the difference between presence and
> absence is great, as great as my feeble mind can grasp. Yet absence im-
> plies presence, absence is not non-existence, and we are therefore entitled
> to repeat: "Come, come, come, come."

Although Mrs. Moore abandons everything, even moral duty, she
dominates the subsequent action. As "Esmiss Esmoor" she becomes,
to the crowd around the courthouse, a Hindu goddess who was to
save Aziz. And, we are vaguely given to understand, it is her influence that brings Adela to her senses and the truth. She recurs again,
together with the wasp, in the mind of Professor Godbole in that
wonderful scene of religious muddlement with which the book
draws to its conclusion. She remains everlastingly in the mind of
Aziz who hates—or tries to hate—all the other English. She continues into the future in her daughter Stella, who marries Fielding

and returns to India, and in her son Ralph. Both Stella and Ralph "like Hinduism, though they take no interest in its forms" and are shy of Fielding because he thinks they are mistaken. Despite the sullen disillusionment in which Mrs. Moore died, she had been right when she had said to Ronny that there are many kinds of failure, some of which succeed. No thought, no deed in this book of echoes, is ever lost.

It is not easy to know what to make of the dominant Hinduism of the third section of the novel. The last part of the story is frankly a coda to the plot, a series of resolutions and separations which comment on what has gone before—in it Fielding and Aziz meet and part, this time forever; Aziz forgives Adela Quested and finds a friend in Ralph Moore; Fielding, we learn, is not really at one with his young wife; Hindu and Moslem, Brahman and non-Brahman are shown to be as far apart as Indian and English, yet English and Moslem meet in the flooded river, in a flow of Hindu religious fervor; and everything is encompassed in the spirit of Mrs. Moore, mixed up with a vision of the ultimate nullity, with the birth of Krishna and with joy in the fertile rains.

Certainly it is not to be supposed that Forster finds in Hinduism an answer to the problem of India; and its dangers have been amply demonstrated in the case of Mrs. Moore herself. But here at least is the vision in which the arbitrary human barriers sink before the extinction of all things. About seventy-five years before *A Passage to India,* Matthew Arnold's brother, William Delafield Arnold, went out to India as Director of Public Education of the Punjab. From his experiences he wrote a novel, *Oakfield: or, Fellowship in the East;* it was a bitter work which denounced the English for making India a "rupee mine" and it declared that the "grand work" of civilizing India was all humbug. William Arnold thought that perhaps socialism, but more likely the Church of England, could bring about some change. This good and pious man felt it "grievous to live among men"—the Indians—"and feel the idea of fraternity thwarted by facts"; he believed that "we must not resign ourselves, without a struggle, to calling the Indians brutes." To such a pass has Christianity come, we can suppose Forster to be saying. We must suffer a vision even as dreadful as Mrs. Moore's if by it the separations can be wiped out. But meanwhile the separations exist and Aziz in an hysteria of affirmation declares to Fielding on their last ride that the British must go, even at the cost of internal strife, even if it means a Japanese conquest. Only with the British gone can he and Fielding be friends. Fielding offers friendship now: "It's what I want. It's what you want." But the horses, following the path the earth lays for them, swerve apart; earth and sky seem to say that the time for friendship has not come, and leave its possibility to events.

The disintegrating question, What, then, must be done? which many readers have raised is of course never answered—or not answered in the language in which the question has been asked. The book simply involves the question in ultimates. This, obviously, is no answer; still, it defines the scope of a possible answer, and thus restates the question. For the answer can never again temporize, because the question, after it has been involved in the moods and visions of the story, turns out to be the most enormous question that has ever been asked, requiring an answer of enormous magnanimity. Great as the problem of India is, Forster's book is not about India alone; it is about all of human life.

CHAPTER NINE

Mind and Will: Forster's Literary Criticism

NO ONE is likely to take with perfect literalness, as representing Forster's actual belief, the religious ideas of the last part of *A Passage to India*. Yet certainly Forster has always had a strong tendency to "accept" the universe and in a way that has some affinity with Hindu religious thought. This tendency must be taken into account in any attempt to understand Forster's mind; it is especially relevant to an understanding of his literary criticism. Certainly it is easy enough, and true enough, to say that Forster is not a great critic. Yet so simple a judgment is not sufficient. It does not take into account the great disproportion between Forster's critical gifts and the use he makes of them. The gifts are great; the critical canon is not great. The disproportion is puzzling, yet we can begin to understand it if we understand something of the nature of Forster's "acceptance."

But first we must remember that all modern critics are judged under the aspect of one of the most aggressive, hard-working and portentous critical movements the history of literature has known, the movement which took its beginnings in T. E. Hulme and has T. S. Eliot as its most notable exponent. No criticism has been so concerned to make distinctions and erect barriers, to separate thing from thing and to make salvation depend on the right choice. Yeats, in one of his autobiographies, says that the religious life consists in making all things equal, the intellectual life in saying, "Thou fool." No criticism has said "Thou fool" so firmly and finally as this modern movement, and in the light of Yeats's remark it is interesting that it has been allied with religion, that it has had the intention (and sometimes the effect) of making non-religious and non-theological thought and feeling seem foolish, unprincipled, and slovenly.

But Forster is impelled precisely in the direction of making all things equal rather than in the direction of "Thou fool," and although he frequently says the latter, he will usually follow it with a quick gesture of deprecation to imply the former. Exclusion pains him and the aptitude for exclusion is what he chiefly dislikes in most aspects of Christianity; the gesture of deprecation seldom follows when a representative of Christianity is the fool. Mr. Sorley, the younger of the two missionaries of *A Passage to India*—they appear but momentarily—considers that in his father's heavenly house there are many mansions and that "there alone will the incompatible multitudes of mankind be welcomed and soothed," and he thinks that the monkeys too will perhaps be included. Yet he balks at the inclusion of jackals, wasps, oranges, cactuses, crystals and mud, and, most of all, of the bacteria inside him—"We must exclude something from our gathering or we shall be left with nothing." And Forster can go so far as to set this down in irony.

But poor Mr. Sorley is right. We must indeed exclude something from our gathering or we shall be left nothing. Indeed, unless we do, we ourselves shall not be left at all. And Forster, after all, knows this and makes his exclusions. Still, deep in his mental life is an aversion to raising barriers and setting up categories. Although he never loses his sense of the difference between sheep and goats, as he grows into life he is far more aware of good-and-evil than of good and evil.

Above his essay, "The Perfect Critic," T. S. Eliot blazons a sentence from Rémy de Gourmont: "Ériger en lois ses impressions personelles, c'est le grand effort d'un homme s'il est sincère." For what it is worth the sentence may be taken as the motto of the critical movement to which I have referred; and although Mr. Eliot, after

The Sacred Wood, would no doubt modify in the interests of tradition and dogma the arrogance of the personal emphasis, essentially it still describes his method. The effort to codify personal impressions is what gives weight and dignity to his work. But it is exactly weight and dignity that Forster fears; he rejects exactly the solemn unity of style that must inhere in the construction of law out of personal impressions. "The human mind is not a dignified organ," he says in *Aspects of the Novel,* "and I do not see how we can exercise it except through eclecticism." Then he continues with a characteristic modification: "And the only advice I would offer my fellow eclectics is: 'Do not be proud of your inconsistency. It is a pity, it is a pity that we should be equipped like this. It is a pity that man cannot be at the same time impressive and truthful.'"

Forster, then, is a critic with no drive to consistency, no desire to find an architectonic for his impressions. We might say of him that he is a critic without any desire for *success.* In short, he is an impressionistic critic. A few years ago the word "impressionistic" was the ultimate condemnation of the critic. But perhaps the long dull battle over Marxist criticism has shown us that one's personal impressions, whether or not one has an architectonic for them, are not things of chance and do not make a chaos. Even if they are not consciously erected into law, they follow the law of the personality, and of the personality shaped to greater or less degree by involvement with other laws than its own and by involvement with desires and intentions: the critic's personal impressions inevitably cohere into a structure.

But if between a critic like Forster and a critic like, say, Eliot, the difference is not so fundamental as at first appears, it is still considerable. For one thing, there is a great difference in aesthetic result. In Eliot the desire to make laws and the conscious effort for dignity have their unquestionable effect upon us. We respond to the effort; the form of dialectic gives us pleasure; we are connected with large issues. Literature thus acquires a magnificent importance, life seems more interesting. In such a critic we have met either an ally with whom we attack some enemy of the human spirit, or an opponent who gives us the satisfactions of conflict. Forster, on the contrary, asks us to relax. He can tell us, and very movingly, of the importance of literature, but he never intends to make any single literary work important. And the manner of his presentation of ideas is personal in a way that mocks the erection of laws.[1]

Eliot, of course, emerges as the better critic. Even if we grant Forster every possible virtue of his method—and it has virtues—he is never wholly satisfactory in criticism and frequently he is frustrating. For example, the essay *Anonymity,* issued as a pamphlet by the Hogarth Press, has a simple and important point. It protests the conception of personality used in the academic "study" of literature and it distinguishes between the superficial biographical personality and the deeper personality which is the actual source of literature. The latter, it says, has something in common with all other deeper personalities and is a "force that makes for anonymity," for great literature "wants not to be signed," but the academic "study" of literature—"only a serious form of gossip"—insists on underscoring every signature. This idea, so simple, sound and right, by a fatal paradox is expounded in a manner in which the superficial personality indulges all its whims; in consequence the idea is not properly developed, or even fully stated.

And not only does an excessive relaxation inadequately represent the ideas, it also leads them astray. In *Aspects of the Novel* there are many judgments that are wrong, not because they have traveled a wrong road but because they have not persevered far enough on the right road: they do not approach near enough to their objects. The

[1] To take a perhaps extreme example, this is the way Forster begins his essay on Virginia Woolf: "It is profoundly characteristic of the art of Virginia Woolf that when I decided to write about it and had planned a suitable opening paragraph, my fountain pen should disappear. Tiresome creature! It slipped through a pocket into a seam. I could pinch it, chivy it about, make holes in the coat lining, but a layer of tailor's stuffing prevented recovery. So near, and yet so far! Which is what one feels about her art." The essay does not succeed in bringing the art nearer; one perceives how useful rigor can be. Forster's Rede Lecture on Virginia Woolf is an act of commemoration rather than an effort of criticism, yet as criticism it is better than the essay; it is a great example of the art of compliment, the greater because it does not try to praise too much. It concludes: "And sometimes it is as a row of little silver cups that I see her work gleaming. 'These trophies,' the inscription runs, 'were won by the mind from matter, its enemy and its friend.'"

estimate of Scott, for instance, is such a judgment; it does not continue through the obvious dullness to reach the rich and brilliant
aspects of Scott's genius, nor does it see over the heads of the stuffy
lordly characters to observe the fine humors of the humble characters. Or, in the comments on Dickens, it is a mere casual conventionality to say that Dickens deals with "types"; obviously people so
eccentric as those that Dickens draws are not typical of anything,
although their rich vitality may bring to mind other—and actual—
people. The division of characters into "flat" and "round" is another
and related conventionality, and an obfuscation of the actual facts
of character-contrivance. Or again, the discussion of Gide's *Counter-
feiters* is insufficient and even misleading. The analysis of Joyce is
quite unworthy. Most disappointing of all from Forster is the treatment of Henry James, beginning with its stale joke about James's
snobbery and his horror of being compared with the shopkeeping
Richardson, concluding with an agreement with Wells's position in
the famous *Boon* exchange of letters, and remarking incidentally
that "most of human life has to disappear before [James] can do us
a novel," that "maimed creatures can alone breathe in Henry James's
pages—maimed yet specialized." Obviously not only energy has
failed here, but with it intelligence.

And yet, on the other hand, *Aspects of the Novel* is full of the
finest perceptions. There are, for example, the remarks on the
aesthetic and moral effect of space in Tolstoy, or on the novelist's
relation to beauty—"beauty at which a novelist should never aim,
though he fails if he does not achieve it"—or the observation on the
"voice" of the novelist, a matter which is never enough, if at all,
discussed in the criticism of fiction, or the appreciation of the inter-
mittent realism of Melville and Dostoievsky which gives their novels
"what is always provocative in a work of art: roughness of surface"
—these are the perceptions of a fine literary insight. Certainly none
but a remarkable critical mind could have instituted the brilliant
comparison between George Eliot and Dostoievsky which leads to
the distinction between the novelist as preacher and the novelist as

prophet. Only a critic truly sensitive to our cultural situation could so well understand the devices of the pseudo-scholar:

This constant reference to genius is another characteristic of the pseudo-scholar. He loves mentioning genius, because the sound of the word exempts him from trying to discover its meaning. Literature is written by geniuses. Novelists are geniuses. There we are; now let us classify them. Which he does. Everything he says may be accurate but all is useless because he is moving around books instead of through them, he either has not read them or cannot read them properly. Books have to be read (worse luck, for it takes a long time); it is the only way of discovering what they contain. A few savage tribes eat them, but reading is the only method of assimilation revealed to the west. The reader must sit down alone and struggle with the writer, and this the pseudo-scholar will not do. He would rather relate a book to the history of its time, to events in the life of the author, to the events it describes, above all to some tendency. As soon as he can use the word "tendency" his spirits rise, and though those of his audience may sink, they often pull out their pencils at this point and make a note, under the belief that a tendency is portable.

Here, then, are the good and the bad. Our final estimate of *Aspects of the Novel* is not, however, the result of a balance of the good and the bad. Rather it is a response to the whole temper of the volume; and that response is genial, admiring, but not likely to be either strong or fertile.

In the same way we respond to Forster's occasional essays. Can we possibly not cherish this judgment of Joseph Conrad?

These essays do suggest that he is misty in the middle as well as at the edges, that the secret casket of his genius contains a vapour rather than a jewel; and that we need not try to write him down philosophically, because there is, in this particular direction, nothing to write. No creed in fact. Only opinions, and the right to throw them overboard when facts make them look absurd. Opinions held under the semblance of eternity, girt with the sea, crowned with the stars, and therefore easily mistaken for a creed.

And we respond to it the more when we go on to read, "One realizes . . . what a noble artist is here, what an austere character,

by whose side most of our contemporary writers appear obsequious."
Yet the essay on Conrad is not satisfying; it has said so much that
it must say more, and it does not.

The combination of particular perception and general inadequacy
continues. Ronald Firbank is not a likely occasion for great criticism
and Forster's essay on him is far from important, but when it refers
in passing to "a hundred other [of Firbank's] sentences or people
(the two classes are not separable)," it touches not only Firbank but
Ben Jonson and La Bruyère. The essay on Sinclair Lewis's development is not sufficiently firm or precise and its conclusion, ". . . The
longer one lives, the less important does 'development' appear," is
not so much disarming as disarmed, yet when it speaks of literary
"photography" as being a pursuit only for the very young, requiring
to be supported by firmer intellectual interests than Lewis has, it is
extraordinarily sound. Or the essay on Proust, inadequate as it is,
contains the comparison of the ideas of Proust and Dante on love,
Proust believing that the more we love the less we understand,
Dante believing that the more we love the more we understand.[2]
The essay on T. S. Eliot is better than admirers of Eliot make it out
to be. Its chief fault—apart from its not pursuing the subject far
enough—is the simplicity with which it views the obscurity of Eliot's
verse, its failure to see that the obscurity is a form of communication. Yet the description of Eliot's prose is admirable—it "conveys
something, but is often occupied in tracing the boundaries of the
unsaid." There is perceptive malice in the comparison of *The Waste
Land* with *Prometheus Unbound,* in the suspicion that Eliot believes
that "the muses are connected not so much with Apollo as with the
oldest county families," or in the reference to the "several well-
turned compliments to religion and divine grace" in *For Lancelot
Andrewes,* and there is sympathetic understanding of the horror
which Eliot perceives and which Forster symbolizes in the cheery
milkman who so casually announced the news of England's entrance

---

[2] In 1907 Forster lectured on Dante at the Working Men's College. He also lectured
on "Pessimism in Literature." The fifth chapter of Miss Macaulay's book on Forster
gives an interesting account of these lectures.

into the war in 1914. This essay contains one of the best possible statements of how literature works to "help" us:

Huysmans's *À Rebours* is the book of that blessed period [of the war] that I remember best. Oh, the relief of a world which lived for its sensations and ignored the will—the world of des Esseintes! Was it decadent? Yes, and thank God. Yes; here again was a human being who had time to feel and experiment with his feelings, to taste and arrange books and fabricate flowers, and be selfish and himself. The waves of edifying bilge rolled off me, the newspapers ebbed; Professor Cramb, that profound philosopher, and Raemaekers, that inspired artist, floated out into an oblivion which, thank God, has since become permanent, and something resembling reality took their place. Perhaps it was not real, but it was helpful, and in 1917 that was enough to make me repeat after the muezzin in my minaret "Thank God."

And five years later, in 1934, Forster comments on Arnold's line, "Who prop, thou ask'st, in these bad days, my mind?" and takes up this theme again:

The people I really clung to in the days [of the war] were those who had nothing tangible to offer: Blake, William Morris, the early T. S. Eliot, J. K. Huysmans, Yeats. They took me into a country where the will was not everything. . . .

All this is fine, yet the total effect is not really impressive. For the fact is that a good critic, as we now judge, is made not only by perception but by belief. It is not that he erects his personal impressions into a law, but rather that he attaches his personal impressions to an extrinsic faith, a framework of tradition and intention which keeps them together and advantageously exposes them to view. But Forster's critical method is precisely the announcement of his reluctance to accept a faith. "I do not believe in Belief," he wrote in 1939 in the essay contributed to the series, *What I Believe*. "Faith, to my mind, is a stiffening process, a sort of mental starch, which ought to be applied as sparingly as possible. I dislike the stuff. Herein I probably differ from most people, who believe in Belief, and are only sorry that they cannot swallow even more than they do. My law givers are Erasmus and Montaigne, not Moses and St.

Paul. My temple stands not upon Mount Moriah, but in that Elysian Field where even the immoral are admitted. My motto is: 'Lord, I disbelieve—help thou my unbelief.'" For belief he would substitute "tolerance, good temper and sympathy—they are what matter really, and if the human race is not to collapse they must come to the front before long."

An inadequate view of things, certainly—the questions and objections that would destroy it will be apparent at once. Here is a liberalism which seems to carry itself to the extreme of anarchy, a liberalism shot through with a sentimentally-literal Christian morality. It is *laissez faire* to the ultimate. In its casual anarchism it is an affront to the Western mind.

But in the odd way that we have, we will feel better and more respectful of it if we understand that it is an entirely intentional affront. The laxness of the critical manner in which Forster sets forth his literary insights is no doubt the expression of a temperament—even of the fault of a temperament—but it is also the expression of an intention. It is *consciously* a contradiction of the Western tradition of intellect which believes that by making decisions, by choosing precisely, by evaluating correctly it can solve all difficulties. In our day it is to be found in such antithetical personalities as T. S. Eliot and H. G. Wells. What Forster thinks of Eliot's Christian society we may guess from a remark or two in the early essay on Eliot; what he thinks of Wells we know from an essay of 1941: "Each time Mr. Wells and my other architectural friends anticipate a great outburst of post-war activity and world-planning my heart contracts. To me the best chance for future society lies through apathy, uninventiveness and inertia."

The vital mess of Gino's room rises to view again—the casual disorder that nourishes life. Forster has many times written with a kind of intense wistfulness of the slovenly East or the blooming tropics or the primitive, non-progressive community.[3] The great

---

[3] In his essay "Happiness!" which is a review of Edy Legrand's *Macao et Cosmage,* in his introductions to Constance Sitwell's *Flowers and Elephants* and Maurice O'Sullivan's *Twenty Years A-Growing,* in his *Letter to Madan Blanchard.*

description of the birth of Krishna in the last part of *A Passage to India* is a glorification of mess and relaxation, of the mind that does not precisely distinguish. For Forster at many moments a cycle of Cathay is better far than twenty years of Europe. Possibly even twenty years of Cathay is better than a cycle of Europe.

Perhaps no one in our time has expressed so simply as Forster the weariness with the intellectual tradition of Europe which has been in some corner of the European psyche since early in the 19th century. The young Matthew Arnold felt, a hundred years ago, much of what Forster feels today. It was the perception of the dangers of a rigid intellectualism, a fierce conscience, the everlasting research of the mind into itself that made the young Arnold keep his distance from his Oxford friends and be aggressively gay, arrogant, frivolous, dandified, at the very time that he was writing some of his best and saddest verse. He feared their nagging, rigorous intellects; he wanted the life of acceptant calm—he never said the life of simple instinct, but perhaps it was that, too—into which the discriminating judgment did not always enter. And in connection with Forster, it is interesting to observe that Arnold found something of what he wanted in the Bhagavad Gita.

In the first chapter of this book I have spoken of Forster as one of the best representatives of the intellectual tradition of Europe. Is it a contradiction or is it a paradox that he should be wearied of that tradition? Neither: it is a modification. In *A Passage to India,* writing of the Indian heat, Forster says that "in Europe life retreats out of the cold, and exquisite fireside myths have resulted—Balder, Persephone—but here the retreat is from the source of life, the treacherous sun. . . ." To Forster, who has so often spoken of the saving virtues of intellect, the intellect, which can be a source of life, can also, at certain intensities, be treacherous. Still speaking of the heat, Forster says, "Men . . . desire that joy shall be graceful and sorrow august and infinity have a form, and India fails to accommodate them. The annual helter-skelter of April, when irritability and lust spread like a canker, is one of her comments on the orderly hopes of humanity. Fish manage better; fish, as the tanks dry, wriggle into the mud and wait for the rains to uncake them. But men try to be harmonious all the year round, and the results are occasionally disastrous. The triumphant machine of civilization may suddenly hitch and be immobilized into a car of stone. . . ." To retreat from the fierce sun of the intellect, to abandon the strictness of order and law may at certain times be the best means of asserting the intellect and order and law.

But even if it is put in this light, there will surely be but few to cheer Forster's retreat from what we think the best aspect of our tradition and the only hope for our future. It is defeatist, it is passive. And certainly if it were generally shared, our situation would be a bad one. Forster knows this, for he is a worldly man. "Tolerance, good temper and sympathy," he says in the pamphlet *What I Believe,* "are no longer enough in a world which is rent by religious and racial persecution, in a world where ignorance rules, and science, who ought to have ruled, plays the subservient pimp." So fighting comes to take their place, and faith turns out to be a necessary "starch." But the weariness remains, and as one watches it in unwearied action, its strange virtue begins to appear.

Part of the principle of the "weariness" is an abiding suspicion of the idea of progress as conceived by historical judgment. In historical judgment itself, as it is usually exercised, Forster has no confidence whatever and the essay "The Consolations of History" represents it, with some bitterness, as but a pleasant academic game.

Yet sweet though it is to dally with the past, one returns to the finer pleasures of morality in the end. The schoolmaster in each of us awakes, examines the facts of History, and marks them on the result of the examination. Not all the marks need be bad. Some incidents, like the Risorgimento, get excellent as a matter of course, while others, such as the character of Queen Elizabeth, get excellent in the long run. Nor must events be marked at their face value. Why was it right of Drake to play bowls when he heard the Armada was approaching, but wrong of Charles II to catch moths when he heard that the Dutch Fleet had entered the Medway? The answer is "Because Drake won." Why was it right of Alexander the Great to throw away water when his army was perishing, but wrong of Marie Antoinette to say "Let them eat cake"?

The answer is "Because Marie Antoinette was executed." . . . We must take a larger view of the past than of the present, because when examining the present we can never be sure what is going to pay. As a general rule, anything that ends abruptly must be given bad marks; for instance, the fourth century B.C. at Athens, the year 1492 in Italy, and the summer of 1914 everywhere. A civilization that passes quickly must be decadent, therefore let us censure those epochs that thought themselves so bright, let us show that their joys were hectic and their pleasures vile, and clouded by the premonition of doom. On the other hand, a civilization that does not pass, like the Chinese, must be stagnant, and is to be censured on that account. Nor can one approve anarchy. What then survives? Oh, a greater purpose, the slow evolution of Good through the centuries—an evolution less slow than it seems, because a thousand years are as yesterday, and consequently Christianity was only, so to speak, established on Wednesday last. And if this argument should seem flimsy (it is the Bishop of London's, not our own—he put it into his Christmas sermon) one can at all events return to an indubitable triumph of evolution—oneself, sitting untouched and untouchable in the professorial chair, and giving marks to men.

In *What I Believe* Forster gave a reluctant and qualified assent to the notion of human improvement—for it is a generous faith. But clearly he has no confidence in it. And that lack of confidence did its useful work when Forster spoke to the P.E.N. Club in 1941 and said that "the past is merely a series of messes, succeeding one another by discoverable laws no doubt, and certainly marked by an increasing growth of human interference; but messes all the same." He was countering the feeling of remorse which attacked so many intellectuals at the beginning of the war, the feeling that if we "had all played less in the twenties and theorized less in the thirties, the jelly of civilization would have slid out of its mould and stood upright in a beautiful shape." He stood out against the mind's harsh rigor to itself which allowed so many intellectuals to acquiesce when *The Times* announced the "Eclipse of the Highbrow." By a certain reserve in his opinion of the powers of the intellect, he could defend the intellect when it was condemned for failure to do what it cannot do unaided.

The impulse toward "acceptance," toward relaxation, had found

its useful expression a year earlier when Forster spoke of the intense
morality, the exacerbated sense of responsibility which he found to
blame for the rise of Nazism in Germany. In 1940, in the pamphlet
Nordic Twilight, he commented on Germany's extreme serious-
mindedness as being one of the cultural habits that made Nazism
possible.

Incidentally (and I think this has been part of her malady) [Germany]
had a deeper sense than ourselves of the Tragic in life. Seriously minded,
she felt that there must lie ahead for herself or for someone an irreparable
disaster. That was the mentality of Wagner, and perhaps the present war
may be considered as a scene (we do not yet know which) out of the
Nibelung's Ring. I listen to Wagner to-day with unchanged admiration
and increasing anxiety. Here is a world in which someone must come to
grief, and with the maximum of orchestration and scenery. The hero
slays or is slain, Hunding kills Siegmund, Siegfried kills the dragon,
Hagen Siegfried, Brunnhilde leaps into the flames and brings down the
Halls of Earth and Heaven. The tragic view of the universe can be noble
and elevating, but it is a dangerous guide to daily conduct, and it may
harden into a stupid barbarism, which smashes at problems instead of
disentangling them.

Still earlier, in an essay in *The New Statesman and Nation* of
June 10, 1939, with war more and more certain, Forster warned of
the danger of the tragic attitude, of the danger of trying to meet the
situation with all one's energy.

The decade being tragic, it seems at first obvious that our way of living
should correspond. How can we justify our trivialities and hesitations?
Ought we not to rise to the great dramatic conception which we see developing around us? . . . Ought we not, at such a moment, to act as
Wagnerian heroes and heroines who are raised above themselves by the
conviction that all is lost or that all can be saved, and stride singing into
the flames?
To ask such a question is to answer it. No one who debates whether
he shall behave tragically can possibly be a tragic character. He may have
a just sense of the stage; . . . but he is not properly cast as an actor. . . .
He will not even pay the tribute of unalloyed terror.

For the effort to meet the situation with what seems all one's perception will actually prevent perception:

We are worried rather than frantic. But worry is terribly insidious; besides taking the joy out of life, it prevents the victim from being detached and from observing what is happening to the human experiment. It tempts him to simplify, since through simplification he may find peace. Nagging and stinging night and day, it is the undying worm, the worst of our foes. The only satisfactory release, I think, is to be found in the direction of complexity. The world won't work out, and the person who can realize this and not just say it and lament it, has done as well as can be expected in the present year. Perhaps the crisis is a temporary one, and now nearing its end. 1940 may bring personal danger and physical pain and new standards.

Personal danger and physical pain will involve the whole of the human organism, will require a more direct, a more organic response than any the conscientious intellect can give.

Forster, then, has no faith in what order the intellect can bring. Many have risen to say that romanticism—by which they mean undisciplined emotion—is to blame for the Nazi ideology. If such futile accusations are being made, someone might well point out that the extreme and fantastic belief in intellect, in logic, in rationality is to blame for the conception of the New Order. Yet Forster, whose first allegiance was to Greece, has a belief in one sort of order—the order of art. The order of art he sets against the order of force. In *What I Believe* he accepts, as any worldly man must, the order of force, and his defense of democracy—the two cheers he gives it—is based on the tendency of democracy to conceal its force more than do other forms of government, and on the permission democracy gives to variety and criticism. The intervals between its displays of force are more frequent and it is in these intervals that the true life of man gets lived and the true work of man gets done. For Forster the truest work of man is art; the order of art stands beside the order of the universe, the best testimony man can give of his dignity. In "The New Disorder" (the P.E.N. speech published in *Horizon*, December, 1941) he says:

[A work of art] is the only material object in the universe which may possess internal harmony. All the others have been pressed into shape from outside, and when their mould is removed they collapse. The work of art stands by itself, and nothing else does. It achieves something which has often been promised by society but always delusively. Ancient Athens made a mess—but the Antigone stands up. Renaissance Rome made a mess—but the ceiling of the Sistine got painted; Louis XIV made a mess —but there was Phèdre; Louis XV continued it, but Voltaire got his letters written. Art for Art's sake? I should think so, and more so than ever at the present time. It is the one orderly product which our muddling race has produced. It is the cry of a thousand sentinels, the echo from a thousand labyrinths, it is the lighthouse which cannot be hidden; c'est le meilleur témoignage que nous puissions donner de notre dignité.

In the pertinacity of art to assert order, Forster says, "there seems to me, as I grow older, something more and more profound, something which does in fact concern people who do not care about art at all." Art is the sign of man's latent ability eventually to make even the right social order. But the paradox is that art which testifies to our worthiness by its order, cannot be produced by social order— for the order of society, however good, is the order of force. And Forster declares the necessity of the artist's being, as the 19th century conceived him, an outsider and a Bohemian. "Order" does not produce order—only the vital mess does that.

The paradox is greater still: in Forster's belief in the relaxed will, in the deep suspiciousness of the rigid exercise of the intellect, there lies the deepest faith in the will and the intellect. Our introductory chapter has spoken of Forster's refusal to be great. It is a refusal that is often disappointing and sometimes irritating. We admire his novels so fully that we want to say that he is a great novelist: somehow he slips from under the adjective and by innumerable gestures —of which the actual abandonment of the novel is not least—signals to us that he is not a great novelist. He is not a great critic, not a great "thinker." He has shirked the responsibility, we feel, and that is wrong in a day in which each man must bear his share. His refusal of greatness is a refusal of will and that is bad. . . .

We judge thus as we see his refusal of greatness quite by itself. But when we see it beside the postures that greatness assumes we find another meaning in the refusal. It speaks to us of a world where the will is not everything and it suggests that where the will is not everything it will be a better and a more effective will. We can see that Morton Dauwen Zabel was right when he said of Forster that "he has no stylistic followers and perhaps few disciples in thought, yet if one were fixing the provenance of Auden's generation, Forster's name—whatever the claim of James, Lawrence, or Eliot—would suggest the most accurate combination of critical and temperamental forces, the only one stamped by the peculiarly English skeptical sensibility that survived the war with sanity and prepared the day for reassessment of the tradition and delusion that made our war possible."

There is a little and quite casual piece that Forster wrote for *The New Statesman and Nation* of November 4, 1939. It was called "The Top Drawer But One." It was about Mrs. Miniver,[4] about whom it expressed a gentle but fatal opinion. *The Times* had written editorials about her, she delighted all middle-class England, and middle-class America even more. Delighted and defeated all of us, for Mrs. Miniver, with all her charm, is the complex expression of the modern will.

Forster begins by comparing her with a certain parson who always had the right cheery word to say to the villagers, who was genial and affable and able to win general esteem. But whenever he left a group of his parishioners after one of his successful conversations, the simple men began to utter smut in order to keep their self-respect.

Mrs. Miniver . . . invites a similar reaction. She, too, has the right word for every occasion. What answer can the villagers make to a lady who is so amusing, clever, observant, broad-minded, shrewd, demure, Bohemian, happily married, triply childrened, public spirited and at all times such a lady. No answer, no answer at all. They listen to her saying the right thing, and are dumb. . . . Even if they disgrace themselves by spluttering smut in her hearing, she is not to be put out, for the class to which she and the parson belong has grown an extra thickness of skin in the last thirty years. "Touchée" she would exclaim, with her little ringing laugh, and pass on untouched. She is too wonderful with the villagers, she has them completely taped. Taximen, too. One day she

[4] Of the book, not the moving-picture.

overhears two ridiculous, fat bottle-nosed taximen talking about the sub-conscious sense. She takes the absurdity back to her husband, whose sense of humour corresponds with her own, and if the taximen had turned the tables and ridiculed *her,* she would have taken that back, too. She has learnt the defensive value of honesty. . . .

Mrs. Miniver is a lady but not an aristocrat; socially she is not top drawer, only top drawer but one. Her ancestry is good, she is very well-connected, but she is not wealthy, she even believes that she is poor and bravely assumes "that she can create the atmosphere of Madame de Sévigné by behaving like Mrs. Carlyle." Like all "the class to which she and most of us belong, the class which strangled the aristocracy in the nineteenth century, and has been haunted ever since by the ghost of its victim," she must assert her class by her will: she lives by the shadow of the past, past manners, past ideals, and her husband, her children, her humor, her intellect and her Bohemian gaiety are the expressions of her subtle will. She represents the way of life, the special hidden vice of the modern cultivated middle class.

It is the insight of the relaxed will that has called the turn on Mrs. Miniver. That, perhaps, describes the limits of what the intelligence of the relaxed will can do—for all the world loves Mrs. Miniver, all the world that can possibly hope to be Mrs. Miniver, or marry her, or be given tea by her. But Forster knows that Mrs. Miniver can defeat anything. He probably even knows that she has read the novels of E. M. Forster and that something of her manner has been learned from their mockery of other manners. In this knowledge he is perhaps sustained by the thought that if the moral intelligence of art does no more than drive Mrs. Miniver from manner to manner, making her not quite easy, it has done its work. Not much to do, perhaps, yet if it did less the world would be impossible.

One has no notion what influence the moral intelligence of any artist has had on the world: such men, for instance, as Dante, Chaucer, Shakespeare, Calderon and Milton—it is with these that Shelley begins a long and famous list—have never effected conversions or made revolutions; yet, with Shelley, we know that "it exceeds all imagination to conceive what would have been the moral condition of the world" if they had never existed. The stories they tell drop deep into the mind of man, so deep that they are forgotten, so deep that they work without man's consciousness of them, and even against his conscious will. A world at war is necessarily a world of will; in a world at war Forster reminds us of a world where the will is not everything, of a world of true order, of the necessary connection of passion and prose, and of the strange paradoxes of being human. He is one of those who raise the shield of Achilles, which is the moral intelligence of art, against the panic and emptiness which make their onset when the will is tired from its own excess.

Bibliography

The following lists do not undertake to be anything like a complete bibliography of Forster. That useful work is the province of Miss B. J. Fitzgerald.

The dates given after Forster's works are of their first publication. The place of first publication, unless otherwise noted, is London. The name of the present American publisher is given in square brackets.

Pamphlets are indicated by †. Lectures and essays which were published first as small books or pamphlets and subsequently in inclusive volumes are not noted. No attempt has been made to list the volumes for which Mr. Forster has written introductions.

The list of critical writings about Forster takes account only of work in English and does not include items which are not likely to be reasonably accessible to American readers.

E. M. FORSTER

NOVELS

Where Angels Fear to Tread, 1905. [Knopf: Vintage Books]
The Longest Journey, 1907. [Knopf: Vintage Books]
A Room with a View, 1908. [Knopf: Vintage Books]
Howards End, 1910. [Knopf: Vintage Books]
A Passage to India, 1927. [Harcourt, Brace & World: Harbrace Modern Classics. Also, Dutton: Everyman's Library, with notes by the author.]

SHORT STORIES

The Celestial Omnibus and Other Stories, 1911. [Knopf]
The Eternal Moment and Other Stories, 1928. [Harcourt, Brace & World]
The Collected Tales of E. M. Forster, 1947. [Knopf]

OTHER WORKS

Alexandria, A History and a Guide, Alexandria, 1922. Second edition, enlarged, 1938. [Doubleday: Anchor Books]
Pharos and Pharillon, 1923. [Knopf]
Aspects of the Novel, 1927. [Harcourt, Brace & World]
Goldsworthy Lowes Dickinson, 1934. [Harcourt, Brace & World]
Abinger Harvest, 1936. [Harcourt, Brace & World]
† *Reading as Usual*, 1939.
† *England's Green and Pleasant Land, a Pageant Play*, 1940.
† *Nordic Twilight*, 1940. [Reprinted in *England Speaks*, The Macmillan Company, 1941]
Billy Budd; Opera in Four Acts, Libretto by E. M. Forster and Eric Crozier, 1951. [Boosey & Hawkes]
Two Cheers for Democracy, 1951. [Harcourt, Brace & World]
† *Desmond MacCarthy*, 1952.
The Hill of Devi, 1953. [Harcourt, Brace & World]
Marianne Thornton, 1956. [Harcourt, Brace & World]

ON FORSTER

Allen, Glen O., "Structure, Symbol and Theme in E. M. Forster's *A Passage to India*," *Publications of the Modern Language Association*, vol. LXX, 1955.
Austin, Don, "The Problem of Continuity in Three Novels of E. M. Forster," *Modern Fiction Studies*, vol. VII, 1951.
Beebe, Maurice, and Brogunier, Joseph, "Criticism of E. M. Forster: a Selected Checklist," *Modern Fiction Studies*, vol. VII, 1951.
Beer, John, *The Achievement of E. M. Forster*, London, 1962.
Belgion, Montgomery, "The Diabolism of E. M. Forster," *The Criterion*, October, 1934.
Bensen, Alice R., "E. M. Forster's Dialectic: *Howards End*," *Modern Fiction Studies*, vol. LIV, 1955.
Bradbury, Malcolm, "E. M. Forster's *Howards End*," *Critical Quarterly*, vol. IV, 1962.

Brander, Laurence, "E. M. Forster and India," *Review of English Literature,* vol. III, 1962.

Brown, E. K., "E. M. Forster and the Contemplative Novel," *The University of Toronto Quarterly,* April, 1934.

Burra, Peter, "The Novels of E. M. Forster," *The Nineteenth Century and After,* November, 1934.

Churchill, Thomas, "Place and Personality in *Howards End,*" *Critique: Studies in Modern Fiction,* vol. V, 1962.

Connolly, Cyril, *Enemies of Promise,* Boston, 1939.

Crews, Frederick C., "E. M. Forster: The Limits of Mythology," *Comparative Literature,* vol. XII, 1960.

—— *E. M. Forster: The Perils of Humanism,* Princeton, 1962.

Deuner, Louise, "What Happened in the Cave? Reflections on *A Passage to India,*" *Modern Fiction Studies,* vol. VII, 1961.

Dobree, Bonamy, *The Lamp and the Lute: Studies in Six Modern Authors,* Oxford, 1929.

Fussell, Paul, Jr., "E. M. Forster's Mrs. Moore: Some Suggestions," *Philological Quarterly,* vol. XXXII, 1953.

Garnett, David, "Some Writers I Have Known: Galsworthy, Forster, Moore, and Wells," *Texas Quarterly,* vol. IV, 1961.

Gransder, K. W., *E. M. Forster,* Edinburgh and New York, 1962.

Hale, Nancy, "A Passage to Relationship," *Antioch Review,* vol. XX, 1960.

Hall, James, "Forster's Family Reunions," *Journal of English Literary History,* vol. XXV, 1958.

Hardy, John Edward, *Man in the Modern Novel,* Seattle, 1964.

Harvey, John, "Imagination and Moral Theme in E. M. Forster: *The Longest Journey,*" *Essays in Criticism,* vol. VI, 1956.

Hoare, Dorothy, *Some Studies in the Modern Novel,* London, 1938.

Hoffman, Frederick J., "*Howards End* and the Bogey of Progress," *Modern Fiction Studies,* vol. VII, 1961.

Hollingworth, Keith, "*A Passage to India:* The Echoes in the Marabar Caves," *Criticism,* vol. IV, 1962.

Holt, Lee E., "E. M. Forster and Samuel Butler," *Publications of the Modern Language Association,* vol. LXI, 1945.

Hoy, Cyrus, "Forster's Metaphysical Novel [*Howards End*]," *Publications of the Modern Language Association,* vol. LXXV, 1960.

Isherwood, Christopher, *Lions and Shadows: An Education in the Twenties,* London, 1938.

Johnson, Elaine H., "The Intelligent Mr. E. M. Forster," *Personalist,* vol. XXXV, 1954.

Johnstone, J. K., *The Bloomsbury Group: A Study of E. M. Forster, Lytton Strachey, Virginia Woolf, and Their Circle,* New York, 1954.

Jones, E. B. C., "E. M. Forster and Virginia Woolf," *The English Novelists,* edited by Derek Vershoyle, New York, 1936.

Joseph, David I., *The Art of Rearrangement: E. M. Forster's "Abinger Harvest,"* New Haven, 1964.

Kain, Richard M., "Vision and Discovery in E. M. Forster's *A Passage to India,*" *Twelve Original Essays on Great English Novels,* edited by Charles Shapiro, Detroit, 1960.

Karl, Frederick, and Magalaner, Marvin, *A Reader's Guide to Great Twentieth Century Novels,* New York, 1959.

Kettle, Arnold, *An Introduction to the English Novel,* vol. II, London, 1951; New York, 1960.

Kermode, Frank, *Puzzles and Epiphanies,* New York, 1962.

Klingopoulos, G. D., "E. M. Forster's Sense of History: And Cavafy," *Essays in Criticism,* vol. VIII, 1958.

Leach, Elsie, "Forster's *A Passage to India,*" *Explicator,* vol. XIII, 1954.

Macaulay, Rose, *The Writings of E. M. Forster,* New York, 1938.

Macdonald, Alastair A., "Class Consciousness in E. M. Forster," *University of Kansas City Review,* vol. XXVII, 1961.

Maclean, Hugh, "The Structure of *A Passage to India,*" *University of Toronto Quarterly,* vol. XII, 1953.

McDowell, Frederick P. W., "Forster's Many-Faceted Universe: Idea and Paradox in *The Longest Journey,*" *Critique: Studies in Modern Fiction,* vol. IV, 1961.

—— "Forster's 'Natural Supernaturalism': The Tales," *Modern Fiction Studies,* vol. VII, 1961.

—— "The Newest Elucidations of Forster," *English Fiction in Transition (1880–1920),* vol. V, 1962.

Mansfield, Katherine, *Novels and Novelists,* London, 1930; New York, 1938.

Natwar-Singh, K., ed., *E. M. Forster: A Tribute, with Selections from His Writings on India,* New York, 1964.

O'Connor, William J., "A Visit with E. M. Forster," *Western Review,* vol. XIX, 1955.

Oliver, H. J., *The Art of E. M. Forster,* Melbourne, 1960.

Richards, I. A., "A Passage to Forster," *The Forum,* December, 1927.

Shusterman, David, "The Curious Case of Professor Godbole: *A Passage to India* Reexamined," *Publications of the Modern Language Association,* vol. LXXVI, 1961.

Stonier, G. W., "Books in General," *The New Statesman and Nation,* November 21, 1942.

Swinnerton, Frank, *The Georgian Scene,* New York, 1935.

Thomson, George H., "Symbolism in E. M. Forster's Earlier Fiction," *Criticism,* vol. III, 1961.

———— "Thematic Symbol in *A Passage to India,*" *Twentieth Century Literature,* vol. VII, 1961.

———— "Theme and Symbol in *Howards End,*" *Modern Fiction Studies,* vol. VII, 1961.

Voorhees, Richard J., "The Novels of E. M. Forster," *South Atlantic Quarterly,* vol. LIII, 1954.

Warren, Austin, *Rage for Order,* Chicago, 1948.

Werry, Richard R., "Rhythm in Forster's *A Passage to India,*" *Studies in Honor of John Wilcox, by Members of the English Department, Wayne State University,* Detroit, 1958.

White, Gertrude M., "*A Passage to India:* Analysis and Revaluation," *Publications of the Modern Language Association,* vol. LXVIII, 1953.

Wilde, Alan, "The Aesthetic View of Life: *Where Angels Fear to Tread,*" *Modern Fiction Studies,* vol. VII, 1961.

Woolf, Virginia, *The Death of the Moth, and Other Essays,* New York, 1942.

Zabel, Morton Dauwen, *Craft and Character in Modern Fiction,* New York, 1957.

Index